JOB

WRESTLING WITH GOD

PAUL STEVENS

12 STUDIES
FOR INDIVIDUALS
OR GROUPS

Life
Builder
Study

INTER-VARSITY PRESS
36 Causton Street, London SW1P 4ST, England
Email: ivp@ivpbooks.com
Website: www.ivpbooks.com

© R. Paul Stevens, 2003

First UK editions © Scripture Union, 2010, 2015
This edition © Inter-Varsity Press, 2020

R. Paul Stevens has asserted his right under the Copyright, Designs and Patents Act 1988 to be identified as Author of this work.

All rights reserved. No part of this publication may be reproduced, stored in a retrieval system, or transmitted, in any form or by any means, electronic, mechanical, photocopying, recording or otherwise, without the prior permission of the publisher or the Copyright Licensing Agency.

Scripture quotations are taken from The Holy Bible, New International Version. Copyright © 1973, 1978, 1984 by International Bible Society. Anglicization copyright © 1979, 1984, 1989. Used by permission of Hodder & Stoughton Publishers, a member of the Hachette UK Group. All rights reserved. 'NIV' is a registered trademark of International Bible Society. UK trademark number 1448790.

Originally published in the United States of America in the LifeGuide® Bible Studies series in 2003 by InterVarsity Press, Downers Grove, Illinois
First published in Great Britain by Scripture Union in 2010
Second edition published in 2015
This edition published in Great Britain by Inter-Varsity Press 2020

British Library Cataloguing-in-Publication Data
A catalogue record for this book is available from the British Library.

ISBN: 978–1–78359–879–3

Printed in Great Britain by Ashford Colour Press Ltd, Gosport, Hampshire

Inter-Varsity Press publishes Christian books that are true to the Bible and that communicate the gospel, develop discipleship and strengthen the church for its mission in the world.

IVP originated within the Inter-Varsity Fellowship, now the Universities and Colleges Christian Fellowship, a student movement connecting Christian Unions in universities and colleges throughout Great Britain, and a member movement of the International Fellowship of Evangelical Students. Website: www.uccf.org.uk. That historic association is maintained, and all senior IVP staff and committee members subscribe to the UCCF Basis of Faith.

Contents

GETTING THE MOST OUT OF *JOB* —————————————— 5

1	Job 1:1—2:10	**Dueling with the Devil** ———	9
2	Job 2:11—4:17	**God in the Dark** ———	13
3	Job 6	**God-Talk: How Not to Be Spiritual Friends** ———	17
4	Job 7:7-21; 9:14—10:7	**If God Were Only Human!** ———	21
5	Job 13:1—14:17	**The Faith That Rebels** ———	25
6	Job 16:7—17:3; 19:23-27	**Our Heavenly Guarantor** ———	29
7	Job 20:1-19; 21:1-16	**The Problem of Pain** ———	33
8	Job 23	**The Silence of God** ———	37
9	Job 35; 36:13-16	**Songs in the Night** ———	42
10	Job 38:1-11, 31-41; 40:1-5	**God in the Storm** ———	46
11	Job 40:6-14; 42:1-6	**The Joy of Repentance** ———	50
12	Job 42:7-17	**Is Faith Always Worthwhile?** ———	55

LEADER'S NOTES ————————————————————— 60

Getting the Most Out of
Job

One thing we can count on in this life is trouble! Becoming a Christian, contrary to what some say, does not so much deliver us from problems as deliver us in them. We still get sick, lose jobs, worry about our children and struggle with loneliness. On a deeper level a personal encounter with God brings, at the same time, exquisite joy and a new set of questions. Sometimes, like Job, we are led through a dark valley without seeing the path out, why we are suffering, whether God has a redeeming purpose in it all and how we are to respond. Are we to just patiently take it all?

Mention the name *Job* and one immediately thinks of patience, partly because of one misunderstood New Testament reference to this Old Testament saint (James 5:11). Job did suffer, but not patiently. He rebelled. Job's saintly friends tried to "explain" his problems by appealing to the logic of good orthodox theology. In the end, Job's almost irreverent appeal to God for an explanation led to his justification and approval by God. While Job's orthodox churchgoing friends were rejected (Job 42:7), he persevered; that is the real point of the New Testament reference. Perhaps, among other things, this surprising reversal can be explained by the fact that Job spoke to God about his suffering, while Job's friends spoke about God to Job. But this is not the only mystery encompassed by this fascinating Old Testament book.

Job raises as many questions as it answers. Indeed, when God finally speaks to Job in the whirlwind (chapters 38—41), God himself asks questions! Traditionally theology has wrestled with how a good and all-powerful God could allow or even *cause* (as Job claims) suffering and evil in the world. Not only are the usual abstract arguments—spoken smoothly by Job's three friends, Eliphaz, Bildad and Zophar—rejected by God and his beloved Job, but they are not even the point of the book.

This is not a book of rational, systematic theology. This is the story of one human being—one very human and very righteous being—who loses his possessions, his family and his health. But it is a story that takes place within the household of faith. And it is faith that rebels and a God who loves the rebel that is the surprise of the story.

In a closed universe (the view assumed by the ancient Greeks and modern secularized people) human beings are tragic victims of fate. In a dualistic universe where God and Satan are equal opponents in the battle of good and evil, one can blame all adversity on the devil. But in the book of Job, as elsewhere in the Bible, God shares his ultimate sovereignty with no one, not even Satan.[1]

Job—and we—have problems with innocent suffering precisely because we have faith in God, whose goodness is known in the land of the living. There is no answer either in jettisoning belief in the goodness of God or in rejecting the hope that *in this life* there should be both satisfaction and justice. In the end, *and only in the end*, Job finds peace with God through his sufferings, and not in spite of them. Ultimately, Job's passion points to the death, resurrection and vindication of Jesus as God's final answer to the problem of the innocent suffering.

The gospel-bearing quality of Job is all the more remarkable because the book may be very ancient. There is no mention of temple, monarchy or prophets. We do not know who wrote the book, when or where the author lived, though there is no adequate reason to deny the unity of the book.[2]

The book contains an astonishing mixture of riddles, hymns, curses, proverbs and nature poems. The introduction (1:1—2:13) and conclusion (42:7-17) are in prose, while the speeches of Job, the three friends, the young man Elihu and God himself (3:1—42:6) are in poetry. No wonder the Jewish rabbis were unsure where to place Job in Scripture. Though they eventually chose the "writings" section, this book fits just as well alongside the great exodus, David and Ruth.

Like all biblical stories, this one catches us in its plot and invites us in its mysterious and ironic way to find God, not in talking *about* God, but in talking *to* him; not in the familiar rhythms of safe theological discus-

---

[1] Francis I. Andersen, *Job: An Introduction and Commentary*, Tyndale Old Testament Commentaries (Downers Grove, Ill.: InterVarsity Press, 1976), pp. 34-35, 64-65.
[2] For date, authorship and textual questions read ibid., pp. 15-76.

sion but at the point of our deepest questions about the meaning of life and of God himself; not in leisure-time spirituality but in the middle of life where it is hardest. "The book takes its place in the testimony of the ages that there is a blank in the human heart which Jesus alone can fill."[3]

Suggestions for Individual Study

1. As you begin each study, pray that God will speak to you through his Word.

2. Read the introduction to the study and respond to the personal reflection question or exercise. This is designed to help you focus on God and on the theme of the study.

3. Each study deals with a particular passage—so that you can delve into the author's meaning in that context. Read and reread the passage to be studied. The questions are written using the language of the New International Version, so you may wish to use that version of the Bible. The New Revised Standard Version is also recommended.

4. This is an inductive Bible study, designed to help you discover for yourself what Scripture is saying. The study includes three types of questions. *Observation* questions ask about the basic facts: who, what, when, where and how. *Interpretation* questions delve into the meaning of the passage. *Application* questions help you discover the implications of the text for growing in Christ. These three keys unlock the treasures of Scripture.

Write your answers to the questions in the spaces provided or in a personal journal. Writing can bring clarity and deeper understanding of yourself and of God's Word.

5. It might be good to have a Bible dictionary handy. Use it to look up any unfamiliar words, names or places.

6. Use the prayer suggestion to guide you in thanking God for what you have learned and to pray about the applications that have come to mind.

7. You may want to go on to the suggestion under "Now or Later," or you may want to use that idea for your next study.

---

[3] F. Davidson, A. M. Stibbs and E. F. Kevan, eds., *The New Bible Commentary* (London: Inter-Varsity Press, 1953), p. 388.

Suggestions for Members of a Group Study

1. Come to the study prepared. Follow the suggestions for individual study mentioned above. You will find that careful preparation will greatly enrich your time spent in group discussion.

2. Be willing to participate in the discussion. The leader of your group will not be lecturing. Instead, he or she will be encouraging the members of the group to discuss what they have learned. The leader will be asking the questions that are found in this guide.

3. Stick to the topic being discussed. Your answers should be based on the verses which are the focus of the discussion and not on outside authorities such as commentaries or speakers. These studies focus on a particular passage of Scripture. Only rarely should you refer to other portions of the Bible. This allows for everyone to participate in in-depth study on equal ground.

4. Be sensitive to the other members of the group. Listen attentively when they describe what they have learned. You may be surprised by their insights! Each question assumes a variety of answers. Many questions do not have "right" answers, particularly questions that aim at meaning or application. Instead the questions push us to explore the passage more thoroughly.

When possible, link what you say to the comments of others. Also, be affirming whenever you can. This will encourage some of the more hesitant members of the group to participate.

5. Be careful not to dominate the discussion. We are sometimes so eager to express our thoughts that we leave too little opportunity for others to respond. By all means participate! But allow others to also.

6. Expect God to teach you through the passage being discussed and through the other members of the group. Pray that you will have an enjoyable and profitable time together, but also that as a result of the study you will find ways that you can take action individually and/or as a group.

7. Remember that anything said in the group is considered confidential and should not be discussed outside the group unless specific permission is given to do so.

8. If you are the group leader, you will find additional suggestions at the back of the guide.

1

Dueling with the Devil

Job 1:1—2:10

When we have hard times we all want to know *why*. More important is the question, *Who?* What we need to know is not whether the universe is friendly but whether there is a friend in the universe.

GROUP DISCUSSION. Before considering the message of this extraordinary book discuss why you think some people who have experienced multiple hardships seem remarkably positive while others whose lives have been uncommonly blessed feel cheated.

PERSONAL REFLECTION. Consider your own faith journey to this point. Was it easy or hard to believe God was *for* you when things went well or when you faced personal disaster?

Is it possible to love God for God's sake, and not merely for the benefits of being faithful, even when there *are* benefits? And what if these benefits are all removed and one is left with no benefit but God alone?

The "upstairs-downstairs" drama of the book of Job starts with a contest, probably in heaven, between Satan—the Accuser—and God concerning the purity of Job's spirituality. God and Satan make an agreement, less like spiritual warfare and more like a duel—with honor at stake and equivalency of weapons. "Downstairs," in Job's world, our hero goes through the loss of everything *except* the ultimate treasure, and even that seems threatened. *Read Job 1:1-22.*

1. What indications are there that God's evaluation of Job—"blameless and upright"—was correct even though he was initially blessed with prosperity?

2. In this very ancient document Satan appears as an angelic adversary with free access to God's presence, unlike the devil in the New Testament. What does Satan accuse Job of (vv. 9-11)?

3. For what good reasons could God agree to a contest that would affect Job and his family so painfully?

4. How would you respond to someone who charges that religion is only for those who can't make it on their own?

5. Though Job apparently is unaware of God's approval, what signs indicate that this is important for Job?

Dueling with the Devil

6. How does Job react to the first test (vv. 20-22)?

---

7. In what ways is Job's response (v. 22) different from responses people make today to life's hard blows?

---

8. As will be apparent later, Job's response included questioning God about the apparent injustice of his situation. What would have been seen as sinful behavior in Job's reaction?

---

9. *Read Job 2:1-10.* Why do you think God agreed to this second test?

---

10. God did not allow Satan to take Job's life. The Adversary attacked Job's possessions, his family and his health. What further attack did Job sustain from his wife (vv. 9-10)?

Why would her suggestion be especially dangerous to Job's faith?

11. Suffering is a mystery, and the opening scenes of this book deepen the mystery by showing how inadequate are our "reasons" for misfortune. What have you already learned about "accepting trouble from God" (v. 10)?

What difference will this make to your own attitude toward hard times?

Ask God to give you a picture of the wonderful pleasure and approval God has for you so that you might grow in confidence that God is your friend.

Now or Later

Job's prosperity is sometimes presented as a *reward* for his righteousness, a matter promoted by the "health and wealth gospel." Abraham, Job and Solomon—all wealthy people—depended on God rather than their wealth (Genesis 13:8-18; Job 1:21) in contrast to those who praised God because they were rich (Zechariah 11:5) but were soon to lose it all.

Study the Bible's message on wealth as (1) a *blessing* (Deuteronomy 30:9; Proverbs 22:4), (2) *a sacrament*, as God gives wealth (Proverbs 3:16; 1 Samuel 2:7-8; Ecclesiastes 5:19; Hosea 2:8) freely and generously but also scandalously even to the wicked (Psalm 73:12-13; 62:10; Job 21:7-21) and (3) *a temptation*, as it provides illusionary security (Proverbs 18:11; Ecclesiastes 5:10; Psalm 49:6-7) as exemplified by the Aramaic word for money, "Mammon," from the same root as "Amen" (see Luke 6:24, 30; 12:15, 33; 16:13; Matthew 6:19, 24).

The health and wealth gospel encourages perverted motives, misrepresents God's deepest concerns for us and misinterprets God's promises to Israel as immediately applicable to Christians (see 1 Timothy 6:3-10).

2

God in the Dark

Job 2:11—4:17

For every ten people who can withstand the temptations of adversity, only one can stand prosperity—or so it is said. When life is good we have no questions, and when it is hard we have no answers—or so it is said.

GROUP DISCUSSION. Drawing on your own life, talk about why you agree or disagree with the statements above.

PERSONAL REFLECTION. Describe an experience in which you were tempted to doubt God's goodness. What questions did you ask? What thoughts, if any, did you have of God?

Job has handled his prosperity as a ministry and later defends his stewardship of abundance (29:7-25; 31:24-25). But now he is plunged into excruciating loss, a living death. Job's new test will examine whether his belief in the goodness of God can be subverted by unalterably negative circumstances. Job will ask questions that are asked in wars and famines, when people are faced with congenital deformities and terminal illnesses. Job will later take up the cause of all the nameless, suffering poor (24:1-25). But in this study Job feels the weight of his own burden first. *Read Job 2:11-13.*

---

1. At this point in the story Job's three friends travel a considerable distance to console Job. What actions of the friends indicate they understood how deeply Job was suffering?

---

2. For chapters 3 through 31 the story moves from prose to poetry as Job's three friends discuss the meaning of his adversity and where—if anywhere—God was present in the darkness. *Read Job 3:1-26.* In what ways does Job's response to his suffering go beyond asking the usual why (3:1-10)?

---

3. Job's chief complaint, to our surprise, is not his material loss but the loss of his spiritual estate (3:25-26). In what ways does this challenge you when faced with discontentment?

---

4. Though Job curses his birthday (3:1), he does not curse God. What is the difference?

5. What does Job think God's role is in all this (3:11, 16)?

6. What new questions does Job ask in 3:20-26?

7. In what ways does Job's speech go beyond the "poor me" complaint so frequently uttered by people in times of adversity?

8. Each of Job's three friends makes a speech with Job responding—a cycle that is repeated three times in the book. *Read Job 4:1-17.* Eliphaz responds cautiously at first and then attacks. Why does Eliphaz think Job is suffering?

9. Eliphaz counsels, "Should not your piety be your confidence and your blameless ways your hope?" (4:6). Is this sound advice helpful? Explain.

10. Eliphaz thinks he has God's word (4:12-17). Job only has dark questions. What have you learned so far about finding God in the midst of pain and loss?

11. How do you feel about living with unanswered questions?

Ask God to show you how to put aside your life circumstances and find rest for your soul (Matthew 11:28).

Now or Later

None of the friends breathes a prayer in the whole book. But Job pours out his heart to God. Prayer is, paradoxically, both a blessing and a battle. Consider some of the many scriptural examples of "taking God on" by righteous men and women: Abraham haggling over Sodom (Genesis 18:16-33); Jacob wrestling a blessing out of God (Genesis 32:22-29); Jesus praying in the garden (Matthew 26:36-46); Paul pleading three times for the removal of his "thorn" (2 Corinthians 12:8-9). See also the Psalms, Jeremiah 20:14-18 and Lamentations 3:1-18. As P. T. Forsyth once said, it may be God's will that we surmount his will. What we mainly "get" through prayer is God!

C. S. Lewis wrote in *A Grief Observed*: "Talk to me about the truth of religion and I'll listen gladly. Talk to me about the duty of religion and I'll listen submissively. But don't come talking to me about the consolations of religion or I shall suspect that you don't understand."[1] What does this quote and these chapters from Job suggest to you about how to encourage someone who is grieving?

---

[1] C.S. Lewis, *A Grief Observed* (Greenwich, Conn.: Seabury Press, 1963), p. 23.

3

God-Talk: How Not to Be Spiritual Friends

Job 6

Mike Mason comments: "The greatest mystery in the book of Job is not why Job suffers, but why a man crippled by suffering is forced to fight a long, drawn-out theological battle with people who are supposed to be his friends."[1] Sometimes people are presented in the Bible—often without editorial comment—simply to show us what *not* to do! Even our worst experiences of friendship do not quench our desire for soul friends, people who will walk with us through life's hardest moments and who will point us to God without preaching at us or judging our spirituality.

GROUP DISCUSSION. Reflect on the friend who has been most encouraging in your spiritual journey. Use single words to characterize your relationship with that person.

PERSONAL REFLECTION. Spend some time reviewing your faith journey from the beginning. As you do this note the influences—good and unhelpful—that friends and mentors have had on you.

"Job's comforters" is the cynical title given to Eliphaz, Bildad and Zophar—and later the young man Elihu. But they started well. Hearing about their friend's disaster, they came to him, wept and sat with him in silence (2:11-13). Unfortunately, the rest of the story is less exemplary, as we shall soon see. In the last study we discovered that Eliphaz's approach to Job was "you are suffering because of your sin or your children's sin." *Review Eliphaz's attempt to comfort Job (4:1—5:27).*

1. What in these verses would have been unhelpful to Job?

2. *Read Job 6:1-21.* Instead of responding to Eliphaz's accusation, Job explores his problem on a deeper level. For what new reason does he want God to end it all (6:10)?

3. When, if ever, have you felt that "the arrows of the Almighty are in me" (6:4)?

What help would you have appreciated from others?

God-Talk: How Not to Be Spiritual Friends ——— 19

4. What word pictures does Job use to describe his friends (6:15-21)?

What do these metaphors mean?

---

5. Do you agree with Job that "a despairing man should have the devotion of his friends, even though he forsakes the fear of the Almighty" (6:14)? Why or why not?

---

6. Is it right to maintain a friendship even if your friend "loses" faith or goes through a period of rebellion? Explain.

---

7. What reason does Job see underlying his friends' failure to minister to him (6:21)?

---

8. What does Job need from his friends in this time of suffering?

Why are his friends apparently unable to help him?

---

9. Later Job will comment, "Men at ease have contempt for misfortune" (12:5). What would enable you to be of help to others in the pit of despair even though you are doing fine yourself?

10. *Read Job 6:22-30.* How could Job's friends have confidence in his integrity (6:29) even though they have no explanation for his problem except God's discipline?

11. What have you learned about how *not* to be a friend?

how to be a friend?

Ask God to show you how to be a friend, to express God's heart, especially with those struggling with affliction. Pray for friends who especially need God's strength.

Now or Later

Scripture gives us some illuminating examples of spiritual friendship, including Barnabas and Paul (Barnabas twice saved Paul for the work of ministry—Acts 9:27; 11:25-26). Explore a positive Old Testament example in Jonathan and David by reading 1 Samuel 18:1-4; 19:1-7; 20:1-42; 23:15-18 and 2 Samuel 1:17-27. Note especially that Jonathan helped David "find strength in God" (1 Samuel 23:16) rather than simply in their friendship.

---

[1]Mike Mason, *The Gospel According to Job* (Wheaton, Ill.: Crossway, 1994), p. 213.

4

If God Were Only Human!

Job 7:7-21; 9:14—10:7

When the bottom falls out of life, we cry: "Where is God when I am hurting? Does he really understand? Can he *do* anything? Does God dwell in heaven unmoved by cries?"

GROUP DISCUSSION. When have you felt angry with God? Did you tell him so or keep it to yourself (or so you thought)? Explain.

PERSONAL REFLECTION. Try to remember your first pictures or impressions of God. Was God distant, close, awesomely different, totally unlike anyone human, or very similar to your earthly father or mother? Explain.

Sometimes the Bible presents the most important truths not in a frontal attack or a prophetic pronouncement, but in a pregnant hint. This study is a case in point. It takes us one step closer to the greatest of all discoveries, the gospel itself—that God should become a human being, making himself totally accessible to his own creature. Job now turns from complaining about his friends to complaining about his God—to God. *Read Job 7:7-21.*

1. In a few words summarize the matters Job raises with God.

Which complaints can you personally identify with?

2. Job is concerned that God will eventually discover that Job cannot be found (v. 8) if God keeps up the pressure. What does this tell us about Job's view of God?

3. Psychologists sometimes affirm that letting deep feelings spill out is emotionally healthy. Is it spiritually healthy? Explain why or why not.

Do you think God gets angry when we speak to him so negatively? Explain.

4. Job believes in God, but he cannot believe God is *for* him. What would Job's suffering be like without a belief in God?

5. Read Job 9:14—10:7. Why does Job feel it is becoming pointless to complain to God (9:14-20)?

Why is it equally pointless to put on a happy face (9:27-31)?

6. What does Job feel is wrong about his God (9:32-35 and 10:1-7)?

7. What specific benefits would Job gain if God were human (9:32) after all?

8. In none of his petitions does Job ask for his sickness to be cured. Describe what it is he wants from God.

9. In what ways has Jesus Christ made Job's deepest dream a reality?

10. When tragedy strikes, what difference does it make to know that God has come in the flesh (John 1:14)?

Ask God to make a home in you (John 14:3) so that through all of life's joys and sorrows, you will know that God is with you, and for you, and in you.

Now or Later

Study the relationship of anger and faith. Later in the story, the young man Elihu will be angry with Job, because he justifies himself, and angry with Job's friends because they justified God by accusing Job (32:2-3). People like Eliphaz think that if they get angry at God, God, in turn, will get angry at them (see 15:12-13).

In contrast biblical saints like Ezekiel (Ezekiel 3:14), the psalmist (Psalm 74:1-11) and Peter (Acts 10:14) "poured out their hearts" to God, the very thing Scripture invites us to do (Psalm 62:8).

Sometimes anger can mean we are outgrowing a concept of God that is no longer adequate. That was surely the case with Jonah who was angry that God did not live up to Jonah's expectations as a just judge of the Ninevites (Jonah 4:1,4, 9).

Mike Mason says, "The difference between believers and unbelievers is that while the former argue on speaking terms with the Lord, the latter do so by turning their backs and giving Him the silent treatment. . . . Anger may be used by God to break up a spirit of complacency. . . . Our anger functions to move us closer to God as He really is. Religious phonies will go to almost any length to hide the fact that their relationship with God is not real or satisfying. But people who truly love the Lord have a consuming hunger for reality."[1]

---

[1]Mason, *Gospel According to Job*, pp. 175-76.

5

The Faith That Rebels

Job 13:1—14:17

Loss of work, loss of loved ones, loss of opportunities, excruciating disease and withering judgments from close friends—these are experiences against which people of faith can claim no immunity. But how should we respond? Simply accept them, fight them, try to ignore them or comply?

GROUP DISCUSSION. In what life experiences have you been tempted to "lie down and take it" and to give up compliantly?

PERSONAL REFLECTION. Consider the difference between compliance and submission. Compliance is a psychological adaptation to pain in which it is easier to "go along with" something or someone than to speak up and face the flack. Submission, in contrast, comes from the freedom of the will, a voluntary, wholehearted agreement with another. Usually compliance is accompanied by a sliver of resentment that becomes, in time, a full-blown depression or revolt. Write down some of your own relational history under two columns: compliance and submission.

Job experienced the loss of everything, even the comfort of his best friends. Yet Job refuses to give in, to accept his friends' explanations, or to accept the absence of God as God's final answer. There is reverence in Job's "irreverence." This study will show us that faith sometimes requires us to rebel—in the right direction! *Read Job 13.*

1. The third of Job's friends, Zophar, has delivered his message. Job knows that the ear tastes words "as the tongue tastes food" (12:11). What message has Job tasted from his friends so far?

2. Why are the friends worthless physicians (13:4)?

3. What do you learn from this regarding caring for deeply needy people (13:5)?

4. How has the well-intentioned "ministry" of the friends driven Job to something more fruitful than mere self-defense?

5. In what way does Job's extraordinary confession of faith in 13:15 prove that God was right in his original assessment of Job (1:9) and so has won the wager with Satan?

6. Job now speaks directly to God in 13:20-28. What does Job request of God (13:20-22)?

7. *Read Job 14:1-17.* What makes Job feel hopeless (14:7-12), even though he claims to have hope in God (13:15)?

8. How does the glimmer of hope in 13:15 compare and contrast with our full Christian hope in the New Testament?

9. If you could speak directly with God, what unanswered questions would you ask?

What unfair experiences would you want God to explain?

10. In what ways did Job rebel in the right direction?

11. What influence has this study had on your own response to the hardest experiences of life?

Ask God to teach you how to communicate deeply and fully with him in prayer.

Now or Later

Research the principle that God's blessing comes not to those who ask nothing of God but to those who will do almost anything to know God. The kingdom is not for the mildly interested but the desperate (Genesis 32:26). Jesus said it is for the hungry, the thirsty, the poor (Matthew 5:3-6) and the bold (Luke 11:8). Job is a case in point.

Meditate on the following passage from the Puritan Richard Sibbes: "Some infirmities discover more good than some seeming beautiful actions. Excess of passion in opposing evil, though not to be justified, yet showeth a better spirit than a calm temper, where there is just cause of being moved. Better it is that the water should run something muddily, than not at all. Job had more grace in his distempers, than his friends in their seeming wise carriage."[1]

---

[1] Quoted in Mason, *Gospel According to Job*, p. 184.

6

Our Heavenly Guarantor

Job 16:7—17:3; 19:23-27

We long to be sure—sure that we are accepted by God, sure that our sins are *really* forgiven (not to crop up again to haunt us like a long-suppressed secret), sure that we will be with God when we die and sure that God is *for* us. Mike Mason suggests that one of our deepest questions is whether God likes us. "Of course God loves us, he loves everybody, indiscriminately, even the people he is going to send to hell. . . . The real question is not whether God loves us, but whether he approves of us, whether we are pleasing to him."[1]

GROUP DISCUSSION. The desire for approval is a fundamental human need. Share an experience in family life, the workplace or church when you felt deeply approved.

PERSONAL REFLECTION. The search for parental approval is bound up with our desire for the approval of God. Reflect on your own family background, experiences of rejection and acceptance, and how these have influenced your faith journey.

Job is wondering what God really thinks of him. As always, struggling toward an answer by talking to God, Job makes another breathtaking discovery, one that can bring life to every other generation. *Read Job 16:7—17:3.*

---

1. In chapter 15 Eliphaz started the second round of speeches, trying once again to cut Job down to size. What words does Job use to emphasize that both God and his friends have become his enemies (16:7-14)?

---

2. In what sense could Job say his "prayer is pure" (16:17)?

---

3. What certainty is impressed on Job's soul as he prays through his tears?

---

4. What do you feel most sure of at this point in your life? Explain.

---

5. Job looks to God for a pledge of security. How is it possible that Job could appeal for help from God when it is God who is apparently attacking him?

6. *Read Job 19:23-27.* Bildad has had his second turn (see Job 18) at accusing Job. What grand assurance does Job's faith now claim?

---

7. In what ways does this great breakthrough answer the deepest quest of his prayers?

---

8. While discovering hope, Job must still exercise faith. Why is it important that the guarantees of our future should still require personal faith?

---

9. There are several images of God's provision in this study: witness, advocate, intercessor, guarantor, redeemer-kinsman. Which one especially gives you hope?

---

10. What difference will this make to the uncertainties you face?

11. What insecurities would you like to bring to your heavenly guarantor?

Come before the Lord, your witness, advocate, intercessor, guarantor and redeemer-kinsman, and present your insecurities, concerns and questions.

Now or Later

Job believes that his heavenly friend pleads with God on his behalf while his earthly friends are doing the exact opposite. Consider some of the same profound experiences of betrayal in Psalm 55:12-14 and in the betrayal of Jesus by Judas (Matthew 20:18; 26:24, 47-48; John 17:12).

Use the following in a time of prayer and meditation.

> The infinity of time and space separates us from God. How are we to seek for him? How are we to go towards him? Even if we were to walk for hundreds of years, we should do no more than go round and round the world. Even in an aeroplane we could not do anything else. We are incapable of progressing vertically. We cannot take a step toward the heavens. God crosses the universe and comes to us. Over the infinity of space and time, the infinitely more infinite love of God comes to possess us. He comes at his own time. We have the power to consent to receive him or to refuse. If we remain deaf he comes back again and again like a beggar, but also, like a beggar, one day he stops coming. If we consent, God puts a little seed in us and he goes away again. From that moment God has no more to do; neither have we, except to wait. We only have not to regret the consent we gave him, the nuptial yes.[2]

---

[1]Mason, *Gospel According to Job*, p. 21.
[2]Simone Weil, *Waiting on God*, trans. Emma Craufurd (London: Collins, 1950), p. 91.

7

The Problem of Pain

Job 20:1-19; 21:1-16

Wars, disease, congenital deformities, earthquakes and the seismic disturbances in our daily lives—all of these leave us with questions about the goodness of God and his active control of the world.

GROUP DISCUSSION. If you have one question to ask about God's management of the world and current events, what is that question?

PERSONAL REFLECTION. What have you witnessed or experienced in life that has made it difficult for you to believe there is a good God running the world?

Job himself suffered economic, familial, physical and social disaster, so much so that he despaired of life and longed for death. How could a good God *cause* all this (as Job firmly believed), or even *allow* this (as most moderns would say)? The classic way of putting the matter is this: If God is all-powerful, he is not good; if he is good, he is not all-powerful. Or "if he is God he is not good; if he is good, then he is not God."

Job will not get his answer in the chapters we are studying. Indeed, he does not get a satisfying theological answer even in the end when God finally speaks—he will get something even better! But his dialogue with his friend Zophar will push his thinking and praying a step closer to the belief that God's love is not confined to rewards and punishments. *Read Zophar's speech in Job 20:1-19.*

1. What words and phrases are used to describe the wicked in these verses?

and their punishment?

2. Why do you think Zophar feels "rebuked" and "dishonored" (v. 3) as, in a previous speech, Bildad felt he was regarded as "stupid as cattle" in Job's sight (18:3)?

3. How would you react if you heard Zophar's theology preached to you from the pulpit?

What critique could you offer?

4. Zophar (and the other friends) argue from tradition, the way "it has been from old" (v. 4). Is this wisdom a dangerous half-truth or a false premise? Explain.

5. *Read Job 21:1-16.* How does Job's reality check contrast with Zophar's view (20:29)?

6. Job 21:14-15 expresses the spiritual question the wicked might ask: "What would we gain by praying to [God]?" On the basis of the discussion thus far, how do you think Zophar would answer that question?

How would Job reply?

7. It has been said that Job and the others were trying to fit together the pieces of a puzzle without having all the pieces. How can the discoveries Job is making (consider the last study too) help Job and us deal with the problem of pain?

8. How might Zophar have responded to the words of Jesus: our Father in heaven "causes his sun to shine on the evil and the good, and sends rain on the righteous and the unrighteous" (Matthew 5:45)?

How might Job respond?

---

9. What have you learned in this study about helping people find answers to questions about the goodness of God?

How have your personal questions been addressed?

Pray for grace and hope as you await the coming of God's kingdom on earth when everything will be fair.

Now or Later

Job has moved beyond contemplating his own experience of unjust suffering to the more general problem: why there seems to be no correspondence between doing good and being rewarded, and doing evil and being punished. Read chapter 24 where Job then takes up the case for the whole of suffering and crucified humanity, realizing that his own situation is the same as that of the poor, the powerless and the dispossessed. Gustavo Gutiérrez notes that this represents a shift in Job's spirituality since "he sees now that this poverty and abandonment are not something fated but caused by the wicked, who nonetheless live serene and satisfied lives."[1] The cruel wretchedness of the poor and the indictment of the powerful in chapter 24 are the most radical in the Bible, though this theme is taken up elsewhere. Read also Jeremiah 22:13-17, Amos 5:11-12 and Micah 2:9.

---

[1]Gustavo Gutiérrez, *On Job: God-Talk and the Suffering of the Innocent*, trans. Matthew J. O'Connell (New York: Orbis, 1987), p. 32.

8

The Silence of God

Job 23

The basic anatomy of the human being is profoundly suggestive: two ears and one mouth. Perhaps we should do twice as much listening as we do speaking. Certainly the friends of Job would have done much better had they listened twice as hard to Job's heart. "If only you would be altogether silent! For you, that would be wisdom" (13:5), said the word-weary Job.

We have all experienced someone's mindless chatter or withering judgment at a moment when we needed to be deeply understood. But when we listen—really listen—we "speak" with our ears. We communicate our respect, prize the person and encourage the movement of God in someone's life.

GROUP DISCUSSION. Recall an occasion in the life of your group when you felt that others truly listened, not by anticipating your thoughts or completing your sentences. Why is this so important in group life?

PERSONAL REFLECTION. Recall a time when a friend or family member really listened to you. How did you feel? How did that person's listening help you?

Could it be that it's the same with God? Does he communicate his love to us sometimes by listening as we pour out our hearts, rather than finishing our sentences for us and telling us how to feel, what to do or where to go? For twenty-two chapters God has not spoken directly to Job. But God has listened in silence. And Job has spoken directly to God, indeed more and more directly. In this study we will explore the connection between Job's experience and our experience of the silence of God. *Read Job 23:1-12.*

---

1. What does this passage express about Job's deepest desire (see also 29:4-5)?

Why does he want this?

---

2. Compare Job's fear of speaking with God in 9:14-20 with his new confidence in 23:6-7. Why does Job now want his "day in court" when he will be judged by God?

---

3. Why do you think Job finds God so elusive (vv. 8-9)?

---

4. Why do you think people sometimes find God unresponsive when they say they are seeking him wholeheartedly?

The Silence of God

5. While Job does not know God (in the personal experiential sense, 42:5), he knows that God knows him (23:10-12). Why is this so comforting (see also Psalm 139:1-18)?

6. Job longs for an opportunity to renew friendship with God and present his case, and he is not simply waiting passively. What has he been doing (vv. 10-12)?

7. How does Job's experience show the difference between a God who comforts through silence and an absent god who is not really there at all?

8. Job thinks of his suffering as a testing not to improve his character (as gold is refined by the fire) but to reveal his righteousness (as gold is proven to be what it truly is—gold). What gives Job confidence that he will "pass the test"?

9. *Read Job 23:13-17.* What appears to be Job's main remaining problem in establishing his righteousness with God?

10. In spite of Job's frustration in getting through to God, Job has not been silenced (v. 17). Why do you think this is so?

11. The Bible suggests that the people who received mystical experiences of God (Moses, Isaiah, John and even Job—42:5) were not seeking an overwhelming encounter with God; these experiences were given by God at God's initiative. What does Job's case teach us about waiting?

How does Job's attitude help you to wait for God?

Ask God to teach you how to wait.

Now or Later

Read and meditate on the following Scriptures that emphasize righteousness by faith: "Commit your way to the LORD. . . . He will make your righteousness shine like the dawn" (Psalm 37:5-6); "Vindicate me, O LORD, for I have led a blameless life. . . . For your love is ever before me, and I walk continually in your truth" (Psalm 26:1-3); "Abraham believed the LORD, and he credited it to him as righteousness" (Genesis 15:6, see also Galatians 2:15-21).

The Chosen is a wonderful novel about a Jewish spiritual journey. It picks up on many of the themes of Job. Here is an excerpt.

> My father himself never talked to me, except when we studied together. He taught me with silence. He taught me to look into myself,

to find my own strength, to walk around inside myself in company with my soul. When his people would ask him why he was so silent with his son, he would say to them that he would not like to talk, words are cruel, words play tricks, they distort what is in the heart, they conceal the heart, the heart speaks through silence. One learns of the pain of others by suffering one's own pain, he would say, by turning inside oneself, by finding one's own soul. . . . For years his silence bewildered and frightened me, though I always trusted him, I never hated him. And when I was old enough to understand, he told me that of all people a tzaddik [saint] especially must know of pain.[1]

---

[1] Chaim Potok, *The Chosen* (Greenwich, Conn.: Fawcett Publications, 1967), p. 265.

9

Songs in the Night

Job 35; 36:13-16

Søren Kierkegaard once said that whatever it may be that one comes to as a matter of course because of aging, it is not wisdom. So we see that Job's three friends, all senior, have tried to explain Job's suffering and to defend God. A tall order indeed, and not necessarily a good thing.

Now a young man, Elihu, comes into the picture. Elihu waited in the sidelines because, as he says, "Age should speak" (32:7). He is also convinced of his own experience of God.

GROUP DISCUSSION. Recall a situation when someone younger than you tried to correct you. How did you feel? What was good about it?

PERSONAL REFLECTION. No one can have someone else's experience. But sometimes people try to use their spiritual experience as a definitive authority for how right they are and why you need to take their approach. When, if ever, has this happened to you? How did you respond? What do you think about it now?

Songs in the Night ——————————————— 43

Elihu is exasperated with Eliphaz, Bildad and Zophar because they have failed to deal adequately with Job. But he is also angry with Job "for justifying himself rather than God" (32:2). So he jumps into the discussion, offering his only slightly revised version of the stock answers. Elihu is given six uninterrupted chapters in the book (32—37) and claims to have a direct experience of God (32:18; 33:4, 14-15; 36:3-4). We will concentrate on one chapter and part of a second. *Read Job 35.*

---

1. What is Elihu's view of God?

---

2. In verse 3 Elihu claims that Job wants to know "What profit is it to me, and what do I gain by not sinning?" Yet Job has never said this. How does Elihu answer the question he poses (vv. 4-8)?

---

3. How would you answer the question on your own behalf?

---

4. Why is Elihu's answer to Job's (presumed) question not likely to satisfy Job, or anyone else in Job's situation?

5. In verses 9-16 Elihu deals with a second question—one that *was* asked by Job: Why doesn't God answer prayer?

What is Elihu's answer to this question?

6. What truth is there in Elihu's answer?

What error?

7. Elihu says that Job must "wait" for God (v. 14). How would you describe Job's waiting?

8. Not all of Elihu's advice is misguided. He does propose that God, if he were sought, would give cheer and comfort in the night when things seem more hopeless than ever (35:10). When, if ever, have you received from God a "song in the night"?

9. Read Job 36:13-16. Elihu is trying to speak on God's behalf (36:2). How does he claim God ministers to people in their suffering?

10. Why does Elihu's "ministry" not offer any substantial help to Job?

11. This study concludes all the attempts of human beings to explain Job's situation and to comfort him. What have you learned about ministering to people in distress?

Lord, I am surrounded by people in pain. Sometimes I shrink from reaching out because my engagement with my neighbor forces me to deal with my own brokenness. And sometimes, like these four friends, I try to "explain" it, assuming a superior position. Please grant me your own tender heart for those who suffer so that whether I listen or speak I may breathe your presence and encourage perseverance and hope.

Now or Later

Read Job 37, the last of Elihu's speeches. Apart from the Lord's own speeches these words are the most magnificent and striking in the book. Note to what Elihu appeals in the wonders of creation and what conclusion he draws from it.

Adolf Alexander Schroeders has said, "My burden carries me."[1] How might this be true for Job?

---

[1]*Die last tragt mich,* as quoted in Helmut Thielicke, *Und Wenn Gott Ware* (Stuttgart: Qwee Verlat, 1970), p. 238.

10

God in the Storm

Job 38:1-11, 31-41; 40:1-5

Surprise is one thing you can count on when dealing with the living God—a tug in the heart when you least expected it, a changed perspective on a difficult relationship with a loved one or a shock of awe.

GROUP DISCUSSION. Share an experience of God that you had in the context of the awesome wonders of creation.

PERSONAL REFLECTION. What life experiences have led you to worship God?

We have had thirty-seven chapters of gut-wrenching dialogue between Job and his friends, heart-rending prayers by Job to his elusive God, and life-and-death questions hurled by Job at God to make sense of the suffering of the innocent. Job, we think, deserves a comprehensive answer from the supreme being of the universe. He gets a surprise. For four chapters God speaks in the whirlwind. This is no "still small voice" speaking. God is thundering. But what he thunders is more questions.

God in the Storm ———————————————— 47

Job wanted acquittal. God called him to worship. Strangest of all—Job seems to be more than satisfied with God's response! Perhaps Job was more satisfied than we are—which is a subject we will explore in this study. *Read Job 38:1-11, 31-41.*

---

1. What common theme do all of God's questions have?

---

2. Why does God emphasize that Job was not around when he created the world and that much of what God has made is neither seen nor used by human beings (38:26)?

---

3. Why do you think it is sometimes more important in our spiritual journey to get more questions than answers?

---

4. Why is it important for God to remind Job about what Job cannot do rather than what he can do?

---

5. What effect will all these questions have on Job's view of himself?

his view of God?

6. Why would it be important for Job to overhear the joy and astonishment of God over the things God has made?

7. *Read Job 40:1-5.* What three words does God use to describe what Job has been doing up until now (40:2)?

8. Describe Job's first response to God's self-revelation (vv. 3-5).

9. Do you think that in every complaint against God there is an implicit revolt against our being creatures? Explain.

10. In what ways do God's questions address Job's deepest questions about God in the previous chapters?

11. How have questions helped you to grow spiritually?

Confess ways that you have tried to control God. Ask God to surprise you with his awesome presence.

Now or Later

Meditate on the following quotation: "The creation of humanity was an act of sheer, uncalled-for extravagance, wholly unnecessary. That is just the way the Lord is, doing nothing out of personal need but only out of His own abundantly overflowing life."[1]

Note the range of creatures mentioned by God in chapters 38—39: the lion (38:39-40), ravens (38:41), the ibex (39:1-4), the wild ass (39:5-8), the wild ox (39:9-12), the ostrich (39:13-18), the horse (39:19-25), the hawk (39:26), the eagle (39:27-30). *Read the rest of God's speech in the storm (40:6—41:42).* God describes two absolutely untamable and awesome creatures—behemoth (40:15) and leviathan (41:1) as though to say "Not only is My world wild but it is wilder than you ever imagined."[2] In doing so God reinforced that the dominion exercised by human beings (Genesis 1:26-28) is not absolute, and we will never control or understand everything. God is God and we are not. "The work of theology in our day is not so much interpretation as contemplation. . . . God and the world need to be held up for oohs and ahhs before they can be safely analyzed."[3]

---

[1] Mason, *Gospel According to Job*, p. 398.
[2] Ibid., p. 401.
[3] Robert Farrar Capon, *An Offering of Uncles* (New York: Crossroad, 1982), p. 163.

11

The Joy of Repentance

Job 40:6-14; 42:1-6

Hardly anyone would speak of repentance as desirable. But it is! Repentance is not joyless self-hatred but blessed God-discovery. Repentance is the experience of coming home.

GROUP DISCUSSION. Describe an experience you had of "coming home." What were your actions, your emotions, your thoughts?

PERSONAL REFLECTION. In his poem "The Death of the Hired Man," Robert Frost describes the farmer talking to his wife over the inconvenience of the hired hand coming home to die. "Home is the place where, when you have to go there, they have to take you in." But the farmer's wife had it right: "I should have called it something you somehow haven't to deserve."[1] Describe your own experience of home.

The Joy of Repentance ──────────────────────── 51

We are now at the climax of the book. Job finally repents. *But of what?* That surely is one of the burning questions evoked by the book, the answer to which will provide a profound clue for our own spiritual journeys. Job is an exemplary saint (1:8) and has thus far rightly resisted caving in to his friends' insistence that he repent of a long list of moral failures. But Job is not exempt from the need to repent, as we will discover in this study. *Read Job 40:6-14.*

---

1. What indication is there that Job has not fully repented even though he is in a more subdued frame of mind and stops speaking?

---

2. What does God say Job has been doing in his attempt to justify himself (40:8)?

How has Job done this?

---

3. In what way can we do this today: to condemn God in order to justify ourselves?

---

4. Must being justified necessarily be a slight on God's justice? Explain.

5. Through what means does God expand Job's grasp of his personal dilemma?

6. God now directs Job to consider two more awesome and untamable creatures (40:15—41:34). Job is moved to full repentance. *Read Job 42:1-6.*

What words does Job use to describe his direct experience of God?

7. What does Job now know about God?

about himself?

about the moral structure of the universe?

8. Job's friends said, in effect, you *must* repent. God takes a different approach. Job was given no direct answer to his questions. On what is his repentance based?

9. What do you think it means for a person to "repent in dust and ashes"?

10. In what way can "despising oneself" be entirely healthy and holy?

In what way could it be unholy self-hatred?

11. What have you learned in this study about true repentance?

Come to the Lord in repentance.

Now or Later

Reflect on the following dialogue by Charles Williams:

> Mornington: "Would you say any kind of curiosity was wrong? What about Job?"
>
> "Job?" the Archdeacon asked.
>
> Mornington: "Well, Sir, I always understood that where Job scored over the three friends was in feeling a natural curiosity why all those unfortunate things happened to him. They simply put up with it, but he, so to speak, asked God what He thought He was doing."

The Vicar shook his head. "He was told he couldn't understand."

Mornington: "He was taunted with not being able to understand—which isn't quite the same thing. As a mere argument there's something lacking perhaps in saying to a man who's lost his money and his house and his family and is sitting on the dustbin, all over boils, 'Look at the hippopotamus.'"

"Job seemed to be impressed," the Archdeacon said mildly.

Mornington: "Yes, he was certainly a perfect fool, in one meaning or other of the words."[2]

---

[1] Robert Frost, "The Death of the Hired Man," in *The Poems of Robert Frost* (New York: Random House, 1946), pp. 41-42.
[2] Charles Williams, "War in Heaven," as quoted in Samuel Terrien, *Job: Poet of Existence* (Indianapolis: Bobbs-Merrill, 1957), p. 238.

12

Is Faith Always Worthwhile?

Job 42:7-17

It is entirely natural to ask in any life investment what we will get out of it. So what do we get out of having faith? Money, power, success, happiness? There are some who would promise that faith will bring prosperity. But life doesn't usually meet those promises. Is it possible to love God without expectation of reward, or "for nothing"?

GROUP DISCUSSION. Consider the difference between a contract (an agreement to exchange goods and services according to agreed-upon terms) and a covenant (a relationship of belonging that is "for better or for worse" as we say in the marriage vows). Share an experience of contract in your relational life, and an experience of covenant.

PERSONAL REFLECTION. How do you react when you hear someone talking about the benefits of following Jesus (such as health and wealth or ecstatic experiences) when you have never received some of these blessings?

Satan's original question and fateful test is designed to see whether Job's faith is without any ulterior motive or, as Satan believes, merely a commercial contract rather than a covenant of belonging. After Job prays for his friends, he has his fortune restored and is given a new family. The story ends with Job living happily ever after and dying "old and full of years." But was Satan right? Is unselfish faith possible? or even desirable? *Read Job 42:7-17.*

1. What do we now learn about God's evaluation of all the characters in the drama?

2. In what sense has Job spoken of what is right about God (42:7)?

3. What difference does God's evaluation of Job make to your own struggling prayer life?

4. Job's friends would probably have agreed with all that God said to Job in chapters 38—41. Why is God angry with them?

5. Note the reversed roles. What does Job now do for his friends that they should have done for him?

Is Faith Always Worthwhile?

6. While Job's case is an individual one (a test case for Satan), what general application does verse 10 have for all followers of Jesus?

---

7. What possible significance can there be in the timing and context of Job's restored prosperity (v. 10)?

---

8. Some people regard the "happily ever after" ending of the story as an anticlimax, unsuitable to the spiritual breakthrough of 42:1-6. What does God's final blessing reveal about Job?

about God?

---

9. In what sense may suffering Christians look forward to the blessing of God?

---

10. How do you think Job would now answer the question "Why are you suffering?"

How could this answer be of help in caring for someone going through a season of affliction?

---

11. What is the answer to Satan's question "Does Job serve God for nothing?"

---

12. How is this question important to you?

---

13. What have you learned through this study about loving God for God's sake?

Ask God to help you find rest in him.

Now or Later

Reflect on these insightful words:

> A true friend can never have a hidden motive for being a friend. He can have no hidden agenda. A friend is simply a friend, for the sake of friendship. In a much greater way, love for God is love for God's own sake. Bernard of Clairvaux wrote that our natural inclination is to love for our own sake. When we learn to love God, we still love him for our own sake. As we grow in friendship with God, we come to love him

not just for ourselves alone, but also for God's sake. At last, we may reach a point where we love even ourselves for the sake of God.[1]

In abandoning now even his need for an "explanation," Job truly believes, more than ever before, in an utterly disinterested way—for nothing. Francis Andersen offers this summary:

> It is one of the many excellences of the book that Job is brought to contentment without ever knowing all the facts of his case. In view of the way in which the Satan brought up the matter, something had to be done to rescue Job from his slander. And the test would only work if Job did not know what it was for. God thrusts Job into an experience of dereliction to make it possible for Job to enter into a life of naked faith, to learn to love God for Himself alone. God does not seem to give this privilege to many people, for they pay a terrible price of suffering for their discoveries. But part of the discovery is to see the suffering itself as one of God's most precious gifts. To withhold the full story from Job, even after the test is over, keeps him walking by faith, not by sight. He does not say in the end, "Now I see it all." He never sees it all. He sees God (42:5). Perhaps it is better if God never tells any of us the whole of our life-story.[2]

Consider the unanswered questions of your own life and how you can walk in faith, trusting God to reveal his purpose at the right time and in the right way.

---

[1]James Houston, *The Transforming Friendship* (Oxford: Lion, 1989), pp. 195-96.
[2]Francis Andersen, *Job*, Tyndale Old Testament Commentary (Downers Grove, Ill.: InterVarsity Press, 1976), p. 270.

Leader's Notes

MY GRACE IS SUFFICIENT FOR YOU. (2 COR 12:9)

Leading a Bible discussion can be an enjoyable and rewarding experience. But it can also be *scary*—especially if you've never done it before. If this is your feeling, you're in good company. When God asked Moses to lead the Israelites out of Egypt, he replied, "O Lord, please send someone else to do it!" (Ex 4:13). It was the same with Solomon, Jeremiah and Timothy, but God helped these people in spite of their weaknesses, and he will help you as well.

You don't need to be an expert on the Bible or a trained teacher to lead a Bible discussion. The idea behind these inductive studies is that the leader guides group members to discover for themselves what the Bible has to say. This method of learning will allow group members to remember much more of what is said than a lecture would.

These studies are designed to be led easily. As a matter of fact, the flow of questions through the passage from observation to interpretation to application is so natural that you may feel that the studies lead themselves. This study guide is also flexible. You can use it with a variety of groups—student, professional, neighborhood or church groups. Each study takes forty-five to sixty minutes in a group setting.

There are some important facts to know about group dynamics and encouraging discussion. The suggestions listed below should enable you to effectively and enjoyably fulfill your role as leader.

Preparing for the Study

1. Ask God to help you understand and apply the passage in your own life. Unless this happens, you will not be prepared to lead others. Pray too for the various members of the group. Ask God to open your hearts to the message of his Word and motivate you to action.

2. Read the introduction to the entire guide to get an overview of the entire book and the issues which will be explored.

3. As you begin each study, read and reread the assigned Bible passage to familiarize yourself with it.

4. This study guide is based on the New International Version of the Bible. It will help you and the group if you use this translation as the basis for your study and discussion.

5. Carefully work through each question in the study. Spend time in meditation and reflection as you consider how to respond.

6. Write your thoughts and responses in the space provided in the study guide. This will help you to express your understanding of the passage clearly.

7. It might help to have a Bible dictionary handy. Use it to look up any unfamiliar words, names or places. (For additional help on how to study a passage, see chapter five of *How to Lead a LifeBuilder Study*, IVP, 2018.)

8. Consider how you can apply the Scripture to your life. Remember that the group will follow your lead in responding to the studies. They will not go any deeper than you do.

9. Once you have finished your own study of the passage, familiarize yourself with the leader's notes for the study you are leading. These are designed to help you in several ways. First, they tell you the purpose the study guide author had in mind when writing the study. Take time to think through how the study questions work together to accomplish that purpose. Second, the notes provide you with additional background information or suggestions on group dynamics for various questions. This information can be useful when people have difficulty understanding or answering a question. Third, the leader's notes can alert you to potential problems you may encounter during the study.

10. If you wish to remind yourself of anything mentioned in the leader's notes, make a note to yourself below that question in the study.

Leading the Study

1. Begin the study on time. Open with prayer, asking God to help the group to understand and apply the passage.

2. Be sure that everyone in your group has a study guide. Encourage the group to prepare beforehand for each discussion by reading the introduction to the guide and by working through the questions in the study.

3. At the beginning of your first time together, explain that these studies are meant to be discussions, not lectures. Encourage the members of the group to participate. However, do not put pressure on those who may be hesitant to speak during the first few sessions. You may want to suggest the following guidelines to your group.

☐ Stick to the topic being discussed.

☐ Your responses should be based on the verses which are the focus of the discussion and not on outside authorities such as commentaries or speakers.
☐ These studies focus on a particular passage of Scripture. Only rarely should you refer to other portions of the Bible. This allows for everyone to participate in in-depth study on equal ground.
☐ Anything said in the group is considered confidential and will not be discussed outside the group unless specific permission is given to do so.
☐ We will listen attentively to each other and provide time for each person present to talk.
☐ We will pray for each other.

4. Have a group member read the introduction at the beginning of the discussion.

5. Every session begins with a group discussion question. The question or activity is meant to be used before the passage is read. The question introduces the theme of the study and encourages group members to begin to open up. Encourage as many members as possible to participate, and be ready to get the discussion going with your own response.

This section is designed to reveal where our thoughts or feelings need to be transformed by Scripture. That is why it is especially important not to read the passage before the discussion question is asked. The passage will tend to color the honest reactions people would otherwise give because they are, of course, supposed to think the way the Bible does.

You may want to supplement the group discussion question with an icebreaker to help people to get comfortable. See the community section of the *Small Group Starter Kit* (IVP, 1995) for more ideas.

You also might want to use the personal reflection question with your group. Either allow a time of silence for people to respond individually or discuss it together.

6. Have a group member (or members if the passage is long) read aloud the passage to be studied. Then give people several minutes to read the passage again silently so that they can take it all in.

7. Question 1 will generally be an overview question designed to briefly survey the passage. Encourage the group to look at the whole passage, but try to avoid getting sidetracked by questions or issues that will be addressed later in the study.

8. As you ask the questions, keep in mind that they are designed to be used just as they are written. You may simply read them aloud. Or you may prefer to express them in your own words.

There may be times when it is appropriate to deviate from the study guide.

For example, a question may have already been answered. If so, move on to the next question. Or someone may raise an important question not covered in the guide. Take time to discuss it, but try to keep the group from going off on tangents.

9. Avoid answering your own questions. If necessary, repeat or rephrase them until they are clearly understood. Or point out something you read in the leader's notes to clarify the context or meaning. An eager group quickly becomes passive and silent if they think the leader will do most of the talking.

10. Don't be afraid of silence. People may need time to think about the question before formulating their answers.

11. Don't be content with just one answer. Ask, "What do the rest of you think?" or "Anything else?" until several people have given answers to the question.

12. Acknowledge all contributions. Try to be affirming whenever possible. Never reject an answer. If it is clearly off-base, ask, "Which verse led you to that conclusion?" or again, "What do the rest of you think?"

13. Don't expect every answer to be addressed to you, even though this will probably happen at first. As group members become more at ease, they will begin to truly interact with each other. This is one sign of healthy discussion.

14. Don't be afraid of controversy. It can be very stimulating. If you don't resolve an issue completely, don't be frustrated. Move on and keep it in mind for later. A subsequent study may solve the problem.

15. Periodically summarize what the group has said about the passage. This helps to draw together the various ideas mentioned and gives continuity to the study. But don't preach.

16. At the end of the Bible discussion you may want to allow group members a time of quiet to work on an idea under "Now or Later." Then discuss what you experienced. Or you may want to encourage group members to work on these ideas between meetings. Give an opportunity during the session for people to talk about what they are learning.

17. Conclude your time together with conversational prayer, adapting the prayer suggestion at the end of the study to your group. Ask for God's help in following through on the commitments you've made.

18. End on time.

Many more suggestions and helps are found in *How to Lead a LifeBuilder Study*.

Components of Small Groups
A healthy small group should do more than study the Bible. There are four

components to consider as you structure your time together.

Nurture. Small groups help us to grow in our knowledge and love of God. Bible study is the key to making this happen and is the foundation of your small group.

Community. Small groups are a great place to develop deep friendships with other Christians. Allow time for informal interaction before and after each study. Plan activities and games that will help you get to know each other. Spend time having fun together—going on a picnic or cooking dinner together.

Worship and prayer. Your study will be enhanced by spending time praising God together in prayer or song. Pray for each other's needs—and keep track of how God is answering prayer in your group. Ask God to help you to apply what you are learning in your study.

Outreach. Reaching out to others can be a practical way of applying what you are learning, and it will keep your group from becoming self-focused. Host a series of evangelistic discussions for your friends or neighbors. Clean up the yard of an elderly friend. Serve at a soup kitchen together, or spend a day working in the community.

Many more suggestions and helps in each of these areas are found in the *Small Group Starter Kit.* You will also find information on building a small group. Reading through the starter kit will be worth your time.

Study 1. Job 1:1—2:10. Dueling with the Devil.
Purpose: To probe good and bad reasons for spiritual life.
General note. In the Hebrew text *Satan* is not a proper name but a simple description of his action: the accuser. However, for the purposes of this study the name *Satan* will be used.
Group discussion. These questions and activities are designed to help the group warm up to each other. No matter how well the group may know each other, there is always a stiffness that needs to be overcome before people will begin to talk openly. A good question will break the ice and help people start thinking along the lines of the topic of the study. Also, these questions can reveal where our thoughts and feelings need to be transformed by Scripture. That's why it is important to discuss them before the passage is read.
Personal reflection. These questions are designed for individuals who want to have a more meditative or devotional experience. If you are leading a group, you could also allow a time of silence for members to pray in this way as they come into God's presence.
Question 1. While almost everyone can identify with Job because his experience

is so universal, Job himself is not everyman. He is a real, though very exceptional human being of whom even God is rightly proud (1:8; 2:3). He can be listed with Noah and Daniel (Ezek 14:14).

Job came from the Land of the East (1:3), which is a general description of the area east of the Jordan. While we do not know that he was an Israelite, he certainly worshiped Israel's God and gained a spirituality that harmonized prayer ("feared God") and ethics ("shunned evil"), both positive and negative—matters to which Job himself (chapters 29—31), Job's friends (4:3-6) and God (42:8) attest.

The reference to "the morning after the party" sacrifice on behalf of his children shows Job acting as priest of his family, interceding lest any of them commit the sin Satan wants him to commit—cursing God (1:11; 2:5).

In his masterful commentary Francis Andersen takes up the relation of Job's righteousness with the doctrine of universal human depravity. Andersen shows that even Job is convinced he is sinful but "it is possible for sinful men to be genuinely good. It may be rare, but it is possible for a man who loves and obeys God" (*Job: An Introduction and Commentary,* Tyndale Old Testament Commentaries [Downers Grove, Ill.: InterVarsity Press, 1976], p. 79). And Job was such a person.

Mike Mason points out, "Being 'blameless' is not quite the same thing as being 'guiltless'. If someone is guiltless, it simply means that he has done nothing wrong. But if someone is blameless it means something far more mysterious: it means that no matter how horrible his offences may have been, all the charges against him have been dropped (Ps 32:2). . . . Our part is to believe this—that is, to be blameless not so much in our outward conduct (though obviously we strive for this also), but also in our faith, our trust in the Lord's faithfulness" (*Gospel According to Job* [Wheaton, Ill.: Crossway, 1994], p. 22).

Question 2. It is all too easy to "read into" this story the Satan who is pictured in the Gospels and as the Red Dragon in Revelation. Taken within the context of this book alone several remarkable features stand out about Satan: (1) His name may not be a proper name but descriptive of his activity as *the* accuser or adversary. Satan appears as a proper name only once in the Old Testament (1 Chron 21:1). (2) He is part of the divine council, the heavenly host (1 Kings 22:19; Ps 103:20; Zech 1:10ff.; Ps 89:7), who attend God but are not his colleagues. Satan is one of the sons of God. (3) Just as there is no polytheism here, there is no dualism—"The Satan may be the chief mischief-maker of the universe, but he is a mere creature, puny compared with the Lord" (Andersen, *Job,* p. 83). (4) Satan has a minor role in the book, not appearing again after

2:7. Andersen says, "It is impossible to believe that the purpose of this tremendous book is to teach us an explanation of evil that Job and his friends never think of, namely that human suffering is caused by the Devil" (*Job*, p. 83). Professor N. H. Snaith summarizes Satan's role as "God's Inspector-of-man on earth and man's adversary in heaven" (quoted in E. S. P. Heavenor, "Job," in *The New Bible Commentary*, ed. F. Davidson, A. M. Stibbs and E. F. Kevan, 2nd ed. [London: Inter-Varsity Fellowship, 1954], pp. 388-89).

Commenting on Satan's question Francis Andersen notes, "Cynicism is the essence of the satanic. The Satan believes nothing to be genuinely good—neither Job in his disinterested piety nor God in His disinterested generosity. . . . Cynicism is studied disbelief; and a mind turned in upon its own malice is the final horror of the diabolical" (*Job*, p. 84).

Question 4. Two conflicting charges are often leveled against believers: first, their faith is just a crutch to support them through life's rough spots, and second, their faith is a fair-weather religion which is untested. When the benefits of believing are no longer apparent, believers will abandon their devotion.

Though the second charge was Satan's approach, both accusations have a common thread: religion is a contract between the believer and God. The believer supplies devotion; God provides benefits. Such a commercial (rather than covenantal) approach to faith is deeply rooted in human experience. But true biblical faith is fundamentally the worship and enjoyment of God because he is God.

As we shall see, Job does not know about Satan's charge, and he attributes to the wicked such thoughts as "What would we gain by praying to [God]?" (21:15). Job's friend Eliphaz, taking up a similar thread, adds that if faith seems resultless to humankind, it is also resultless to God: "What pleasure would it give the Almighty if you were righteous?" (22:3). Both are probing the question behind the questions, "Why trust God?" This question will be answered in this book not by a rational argument but by truth strained through the experience of one exceptional human being.

The nature of the struggle is complex indeed. The action of Satan takes place in the presence of God, but we are not told where. The real contest is not between Satan and Job (spiritual warfare of a human being with the devil) but between God and Satan.

Mike Mason says, "It is a celestial battle, fought on earth, a sort of duel between good and evil" so that "human beings, soul and body, are the dueling ground where the heavenly powers clash" ("The Wizard of Uz: Meditations on Job," *Crux* 27 [June 1991]: 37). He suggests that a duel is a better metaphor for the conflict than spiritual warfare since God could have blasted his puny Satan, but in a duel, equivalent weapons are chosen and the contest is kept *fair.* God's omnipotence is never in question. "But what is being disputed in dubious battles on earth is God's moral *right* to omnipotence, his mandate to rule" (Mason, "Wizard," p. 38).

So there is a contest which is not exactly a wager because there are no stakes. In this contest it turns out that God knows his Job better than Satan does—which is no small comfort to the rest of us. Untested faith is immature faith (Jas 1:2-8), and we have a God who takes risks with those he loves. Some sicknesses or disasters may be God's permissive will allowed for some greater good now hidden from our eyes, as it was (initially) hidden from Job.

Question 5. Not only is the purpose of the duel kept from Job, but so is God's unqualified admiration of Job, until the end (42:7). Though it will be clear from Job's agonizing prayers that follow, both he and we long for God's approval more than anything.

The basic questions of the book are now before us: "Is God so good he can be loved for Himself, not just for his gifts? Can a man hold on to God when there are no benefits attached?" (Andersen, p. 85).

Question 6. For Job—as well as many believers—faith does not reduce the suffering but rather causes it. Job responds in faith not only by showing the culturally appropriate outer signs of grief and bereavement, but by worshiping God inwardly by seeing God's hand in it all, though he knows not why. Job honors God and his blessings even when circumstances appear to shout the denial of the goodness of God.

Question 7. The secularist, the fatalist, the atheist and the hedonist do not have Job's problem, but neither will they have his ultimate blessing (42:5). Others will talk about their rights and so charge God with wrongdoing, but Job believes God to be absolutely sovereign. Those pressing their rights reject creatureliness (and their Creator) and thus find life to be ultimately tragic. In contrast, by accepting creatureliness and the Sovereign Lord, Job can live in hope even while contemplating his own death.

Question 9. See the notes on questions 3 and 4 for the issues surrounding the first test. Though the Lord says in 2:3 that he has ruined Job "without any reason," there *was* a reason in the first test: to prove Satan wrong and to prove Job right. But the Hebrew word here also means "futile" or "in vain," which may be closer to the true meaning: Satan has got nowhere with God or Job.

Satan's first round in the contest has failed, so now he proposes the loss of Job's health. Later references highlight some of the symptoms of Job's unnamed disease: emaciation (19:20), fever (30:30), depression (7:16; 30:15), weeping (16:16), sleeplessness (7:4), nightmares (7:14), bad breath

(19:17), failing vision (16:16) and rotting teeth (19:20). Sitting on the ash heap—now an obvious outcast from the community—Job, according to the Greek translation of the book, used a potsherd to scrape the pus off his sores.

God is still in charge, however, and Job's life must be spared (2:6). Even in this God would not allow his beloved creature to be tempted above what he was able to stand (1 Cor 10:13). Job, as we will soon see, longed for death as a way of escape, but God provided another way.

Derek Kidner comments helpfully of the morality of the contest and suggests that this concession to Satan was not merely an isolated tactic but a consistent practice. "God's chosen way was not to crush (evil) out of hand but to wrestle with it; and to do so in weakness rather than in strength, through men more often than through miracles, and through costly permissions rather than through flat refusals . . . overcoming it in fair combat, not by veto but by hard-won victory" (*The Wisdom of Proverbs, Job & Ecclesiastes* [Downers Grove, Ill.: InterVarsity Press, 1985], p. 59).

Question 10. Literally becoming Satan's advocate, Job's wife proposed that her husband do exactly what Satan had predicted. Apparently, in questioning whether Job's faith has done any good for him, she had already lost her faith and wanted her husband to join her as Eve does with Adam (Gen 3:1-6). Though in the first temptation the issue was the presumed *benefits* of rejecting single-minded obedience (Gen 3:5); in this case the issue was the apparent *nonbenefit* of believing. In both Genesis and Job the issue is that faith must not be not founded on personal gain or disqualified by personal loss.

In spite of his wife's provocation, and later his friends', Job *refused* to sin by cursing God through insisting on his own rights. As Andersen shows (*Job*, p. 93), Job responds to the first contest by insisting it is equally right for God to give gifts and to retrieve them, and to the second contest by insisting it is equally right for God to send good or bad and to do so without attributing wickedness in God. Adding to Job's suffering is the breakdown of all intimate relationships including, as we will see, that with his friends.

Question 11. A remarkable commentary on Job by a South American theologian suggests that the West has not had a theology of the evil of misfortune, the evil suffered by the innocent, no-fault suffering. Gustavo Gutiérrez, speaking of the final "answer" given to Job about his suffering by the Lord in the whirlwind speech, says, "The truth [Job] has grasped and that has lifted him to the level of contemplation is that justice alone does not have the final say about how we are to speak of God. Only when we have come to realize that God's love is freely bestowed do we enter fully and definitively into the God of faith" (*On Job: God-Talk and the Suffering of the Innocent*, trans. Matthew J. O'Connell [New York: Orbis, 1987], p. 87). God's love—and true faith—does not operate in a world of cause and effect, but in freedom and grace.

Study 2. Job 2:11—4:17. God in the Dark.
Purpose: To find responses to suffering that are helpful and honoring to God.
Question 4. In cursing the day of his birth Job is not cursing the God who so marvelously created him. Job 10:8 attributes to God both the physical shaping of his life, with a possible allusion to sperm in 10:10, and the moral formation of his personhood (10:12). Yet he also says that he loathes his life (10:1), wishes he were never born, had died at birth (3:11) or could die now (3:11-19). He curses neither God nor himself. Later Job will question God, but for the moment he moans (3:24-26) about his own miserable and apparently cursed existence. God may be responsible but God's goodness is not in question—not yet!

Question 5. As Job pounds out his complaint, he does so *both*—as will be apparent even more in later speeches—to God and to his friends. The speeches from chapters 3—31 have a unique character. They are not merely dramatic speeches in a play. This is not merely an intellectual exercise or a debate. It is hard even to characterize the "positions" of Job's three friends. And the conversation of Job and his friends is not truly a dialogue. Job's friends are trying to make their points, usually in line with conventional religious maxims such as "God gives people what they deserve." On the other hand, Job, rejecting the conventional wisdom, tries to make sense of his life by talking to himself, to his friends and supremely to his God, making him "the only authentic theologian in the book" (Andersen, *Job,* p. 98).

Questions 6-7. While Job considers what it would be like if he did not exist, or never had, he also takes up the case for all of humanity—for those who seem to be born for trouble. One thinks of the poorest of the poor, those born and raised in concentration camps and refugee villages, who grow up to be a despised minority, who never receive advantages, whose life appears to be senseless and meaningless, who just survive. Is Job's suffering greater because he has known prosperity, known joy, known the presence of God? In this book suicide is never contemplated because, presumably, death as well as life must be God's gift. What bothers Job is not only the physical suffering but the spiritual darkness, experiencing the absence of God (see 29:2-3) and feeling hedged in by God (3:23). God is absent in the way he has known in the past (as friend), and he is present as enemy! Job's passionate outburst against God's negative involvement in his life hints that the godly way may not always be to make reason triumph over passion, or to have "a stiff upper lip." Job is in line with the Psalms, Jeremiah 20:14-18, Lamentations 3:1-18 and the agony of Jesus (Mt 27:46). He "tells it all" to God in the presence of his friends. This is not only emotionally healthy but a key to Job's perseverance (Jas 5:11).

Question 8. Eliphaz tries to encourage Job, but he does so by insisting Job "practice what he has preached," so rendering his present discouragement morally wrong. He accuses Job of not *feeling* differently. Instead of letting Job have his own experience, Eliphaz and the others try to encourage by giving reasonable answers to Job's questions. Eliphaz's logic is straightforward: sinners suffer consequences (4:7-11); Job is suffering; therefore Job is a sinner. Eliphaz calls Job to appeal to God (5:8—the very thing he will do) and to accept the "blessing" of the Lord's correction and discipline (5:17) because God not only wounds but heals (5:18). Cold comfort indeed.

In contrast God (in this book) encourages by his silence, and ultimately by giving Job the big view—expanding his vision to have a God-sized view of reality. Ironically, God's nonanswer to Job's discouragement incited Job to prayer; the friends' verbal approach incited Job to self-justification. Again, ironically, the friends' accusations forced Job to stumble on some good news—Job is accepted by God not because of his impeccable record but because of his faith—justification by faith alone.

Questions 9-10. Eliphaz operates on a widely held universal principle that moral effort is worthwhile, and immorality results in suffering (4:8). He and his friend conclude from this that Job must be suffering because he is a sinner. Job, therefore, must conclude that, because he is convinced of his innocence, God is unjust. Eliphaz's appeal to Job's faith involves admitting his sin and turning to God; Job's faith leads him to question God. Eliphaz maintains that God's ways are beyond ours, inscrutable (5:9). Eliphaz uses the mystery of God to prove he is right and Job is wrong—you can't understand it, so why don't you just accept it? Job later comes to the same conclusion but as a matter of faith. Eliphaz reveals that the real authority for his ministry to his friend is not in God but in his own theology. He has God under control even though he claims that God dwells in a mystery. It is another great irony that Job's piety *was* his confidence, but for reasons different from those proposed by Eliphaz and his friends.

Francis Andersen offers a helpful New Testament perspective on the matter under discussion—whether good and bad get what they deserve: "Paul makes clear what Job gropes after. This faith will be broken by life, unless it is held eschatologically, in hope; for the 'harvest is the close of the age' (Mt.

13:39), and Eliphaz's truth will be seen only 'on that day when . . . God judges the secrets of men by Christ Jesus' (Rom. 2:16)" (Job, p. 113).

Study 3. Job 6. God-Talk: How Not to Be Spiritual Friends.
Purpose: To understand some dimensions of spiritual friendship through concrete examples.
General note. The concept of "spiritual friend" may be a new one. Simply put, a spiritual friend is another person who walks with you on your spiritual journey, encouraging you in your life of faith, fanning the coals of your passion for God, listening to your heart, cultivating the life of prayer. Spiritual friendship is not counseling, not directing, not judging, not teaching. It is a side-by-side relationship of trust in which each can tell an unedited version of one's inner life, and do so in the presence of God for mutual upbuilding. Tragically, most followers of Christ today do not have such relationships, even in the church!
Question 1. Eliphaz starts with some discretion (4:2) but then seems to unload his pent-up frustration and anger. Instead of continuing to listen, Eliphaz attacks. He claims to point Job toward God ("I would appeal to God," 5:8) and exhorts him to hold on to God's promise of blessing and healing (5:17-19).

Job is grieved and hurt by his friends and eventually becomes irritated and angry. His only hope in the end is in God, to whom he continuously turns, but more *in spite of* the spiritual help of his friends than because of it! In particular Job 5:9-27 shows that Eliphaz views God as awesome, holy, manifestly just in all his dealings with the evildoers (vv. 12-13), compassionate with the poor (vv. 15-16) and gracious to the person (like Job) who is being corrected (vv. 17-26). Eliphaz ends his speech from a presumed superior spiritual position (v. 27). His nonhelp is related to his view of God, his view of Job, his understanding of divine chastisement and his view of himself.

Reflecting on the book as a study in pastoral care, William Hulme says: "Eliphaz' purpose is to shame Job into silence. If we can make a person feel guilty, we can control him. This is the most effective kind of domination because it is domination from within the person. By manipulating his conscience we can tyrannize his spirit" (*Dialogue in Despair* [Nashville: Abingdon, 1968], p. 28).
Question 2. Job feels that God is against him, even more, that God is picking him out for target practice (6:4). As he sees it, if God is responsible for everything, then God must be the cause. Coming as many do from a society that is essentially secular, we may find this hard to grasp. The alternative—that God is not directly responsible and is helpless before a fateful process outside his

control—has greater problems. Another alternative would be to see it as God's choice not to intervene—also troubling to the person suffering.

Job's request that God would crush him to death is tied to the expected consolation that he had "not denied the words of the Holy One" (v. 10). Job is still righteous, but he does not know whether he can hold on. He would rather die now than lose his spiritual integrity. All of this is said as a prayer to God even though Job speaks about God in the third person—a conventional manner of speaking respectfully to a superior (Andersen, *Job*, p. 129). Job speaks *to* God (for example, directly in 7:7-21); his friends speak *about* God. His friends would have been better to talk to God about their friend rather than talking about God to Job.

Question 4. The metaphors pile up images of frustrated hope for help. The word pictures find their origin in the waters of Israel that can be dry one day, a roaring stream the next and then dry again—frustrating weary travelers counting on refreshment. Job himself eventually categorizes his friends as "miserable comforters" (16:2). But the book does not picture Job's friends as hypocrites or heretics. In fact some of Eliphaz's words are quoted in the New Testament as inspired Scripture (5:13 in 1 Cor 3:19; 5:17 and in Heb 12:5). Derek Kidner comments that "the basic error of Job's friends is that they overestimate their grasp of truth, misapply the truth they know, and close their minds to any facts that contradict what they assume" (Kidner, *The Wisdom*, p. 61). What kept them from being soul friends was not false doctrine but theological arrogance.

Question 5. Verse 14 is notoriously difficult to translate, and commentators (see Andersen, *Job*, p. 130 and H. H. Rowley, *The Book of Job*, New Century Bible Commentary [Grand Rapids, Mich.: Eerdmans, 1970], pp. 61-62) cannot agree whether it is Job or Eliphaz who is forsaking the fear of the Lord by failing to show covenant loyalty (*kindness*)—Job by failing in his personal loyalty to God or Eliphaz in failing to show kindness to his friend. The RSV translates the verse "He who withholds kindness from a friend forsakes the fear of the Almighty." Either way, Job is registering the failure of his friend to show him kindness at his moment of need, a matter which Job claimed his own religion considered fundamental (29:12-17).

Question 6. Like Eliphaz, we struggle to remain affectionately loyal (two dimensions implied in covenant love) with people close to us when they cannot embrace our view of God's ways, or they go through a dark night of the soul. It is all too easy to avoid relationship with a person who, we suspect, is under the displeasure of God. Sometimes we fear being polluted by association. Paul dealt in the New Testament with a different though related circumstance of a believing wife finding herself in a covenant with an unbelieving husband (1 Cor 7:12-14). Paul pointed to the positive influence which the believer can give—as Peter advises, an influence to be expressed in life rather than sermons (1 Pet 3:1-2).

Questions 7-8. The progression of the friends' attacks can be traced through the book. After finding Job unwilling to accept the idea that his suffering was because of personal sin, the friends move from gently probing for secret sins to outright attack (chapter 15). In language reminiscent of the suffering servant, Job can cry, "Men open their mouths to jeer at me, they strike my cheek in scorn and unite together against me" (16:10; compare with Is 50:6; 53:3). The friends invent a list of terrible sins that they claim he must have committed (Job 22:5-11) in their attempt to defend the justice and honor of God. This is an action often taken by zealous defenders of God, but it is soundly denounced not only by Job (13:7-9) but by God (42:7).

The reasons for their misguided, unkind strategy are not only a failure in their own faith—a failure to welcome and to live with mystery—but their own insecurities. Sprinkled throughout the dialogues are Job's assessments of the real reasons for the attacks of the friends: his disaster awakened fear in them, perhaps that something dreadful could happen to them (6:21); they felt superior (12:5; 13:2); and they felt their honor was threatened by Job's protestations (18:3) and rebukes (20:3). Eventually, Elihu will vindictively pray, "Oh, that Job might be tested to the utmost" (34:36).

One of the great challenges of spiritual friendship is to welcome our friends as they are, even when we have no explanation for their experience, and there is nothing we can *do* to change their situation. What we can do is create a space in our hearts where they can be free. Without such inspired hospitality we may try to control the person when we cannot explain their experience. Those wishing to explore the pastoral implications of the dialogues may consult William E. Hulme's *Dialogue in Despair.*

Question 9. Commenting on 12:5, Rowley says, "Job is observing that the theology of the friends is the theology of the prosperous, who can afford to look down on the unfortunate and excuse themselves from giving sympathy by the assumption that they have brought it upon themselves" (*Book of Job,* p. 92). Job himself, once a prosperous man, did not allow his wealth to insulate him from the poor and powerless (29:12-17), and even now—perhaps because of this—in his extreme suffering and loss he takes up the cause of suffering humanity (24:1-25).

Though this is not the message of the book of Job, the Bible does suggest that the rich need the poor and that some form of voluntary impoverishment is crucial to the true godliness of the rich, a matter which Job apparently understood intuitively. The importance of this for soul friends cannot be overstated. Compassion shown in times of relative prosperity—whether material or spiritual—prepares us to give and receive compassion in times of poverty and need—whether material or spiritual.

Question 10. The NIV text note suggests that *integrity* (v. 29) could also be translated *righteousness*. This brings us again to the heart of the matter. God is convinced Job is a righteous man (1:8). Satan admits Job is righteous, but questions whether it is *disinterested* righteousness. The friends, operating from their cause-effect theology, cannot believe Job could be righteous while suffering the obvious displeasure of God. Job is adamant: he knows he is not suffering because he is a sinner, and he knows he has integrity before God. Ironically, his friends' accusations and his own internal witness to being righteous will drive him not to mere self-justification but to a discovery of the gospel in the Old Testament.

Study 4. Job 7:7-21; 9:14—10:7. If God Were Only Human!

Purpose: To explore the meaning of the Incarnation—that God should become a human being.

General note. For some people the humanity of God is precisely their problem—God is pictured as a projection of their earthly father or mother, often making belief emotionally intolerable and spiritually paralyzing. In the end we are not *convinced* about the fatherhood of God (by reflecting on our experience of being parented) but *converted* to it. Other people will, like Job, struggle with God's absolute transcendence, making God unapproachable and unknowable. Christians claim that the problem of imagining God is answered by the Incarnation (God's having revealed himself through a complete human life). God has made himself known, whispering baby talk to our ears, yet not in such an overwhelming way that the need for faith is eliminated.

Questions 1-2. Job's complaints make an impressive list: (1) his life is too short for God to make all this happen to him, (2) God will look for him and miss him when he finally dies, (3) he doesn't want to live this way forever and doesn't *want* eternal life if this is what it will be like, (4) he feels God is using him for target practice, and (5) when it is all over God will look for him and be disappointed that Job is no more.

Scholars are uncertain whether verses 17-19 are a parody on Psalm 8 or whether Job's "hymn" came first. Instead of rejoicing (as Psalm 8 does) in the amazing concern of God for his human creature, Job feels that God is the heavenly inspector. So Job wants some privacy (7:19), at least for a breather. Going deeper still, Job wants to know why God has not forgiven him *if* he is still in sin (v. 21). As Andersen says, "The reader knows that this stand of Job is entirely correct. His sufferings are so beyond the proportion of any sin he knows of that there must be some explanation beyond the categories of sin and punishment" (*Job*, p. 139).

Question 3. In contrast to Eliphaz, who believes that prayer is pointless because no one is listening (5:1), Job believes he is not a *mere* creature but a person lovingly and awesomely created by the living God (10:8-12). So he insists on the "right" of asking his questions directly to God even if the questions are unanswerable, as it turns out they largely are. But this questioning is not merely therapeutic. It is spiritually productive, because Job's highest desire is not merely for answers but for the "friendship of God" (29:4).

Pleading his case as boldly and artlessly as he does, Job reveals a heart determined to find meaning. The preacher in Ecclesiastes 1:1-2, in contrast, also judged life to be futile but got mired in sourness, in part because he did not pursue his questions, as Job did, to their final answer (Andersen, *Job*, p. 134). Perhaps bad prayers are better than no prayers.

God's final revelation to Job in chapters 38—41 does not contain a criticism of Job's prayer life, though God does accuse Job of condemning God in order to justify himself (40:8). God (astonishingly) says that Job has spoken well of his creator (42:7). What God criticizes and what Job must repent of is a subject of a later study.

Question 4. Job has not yet concluded that this negative attention from God is better than no *attention* at all, or experiencing deep suffering without any reference to God at all. Superficially, one might think it makes it *easier* to believe in the goodness of God if God is not *directly* responsible for everything bad that "happens." But then God would not be the author of good. In the end, as we shall see, the answer will lie beyond simple cause-effect. True faith in God will not be under human rational control. It is wholehearted abandon to God that is almost violent in nature because of its intensity (Mt 11:12). Job has such faith—as will soon be apparent—and God will approve of his faith.

Question 5. In chapter 9 Job stumbles on the folly of hoping in a God-man. But his reasons are largely negative. In the first section (9:2-13) he complains God is *arbitrary*—omnipotent in nature (9:5-10) and not controlled in anger (9:13). Then (9:14-24) Job claims God is *elusive*—whether God summons Job (9:14-15) or Job summons God (9:16-20), God will likely discriminate in favor of the wicked. Though if he believes he is truly innocent he would, if given an audience, end up condemning himself in the presence of such an awesome judge (9:20). Finally (9:25—10:7), Job concludes that his plight is hopeless because God is *inhumane*. A just decision is impossible because Job is human and God is not. But if God were human, Job would have an accessible God and a friendship with God—something for which Job longed even more than justice (23:3; 29:4).

Questions 6-7. Job's problem is complex. He is convinced simultaneously that he is innocent and that God holds him guilty (9:29). So Job explores his need for a mediator ("someone to arbitrate between us," 9:33), a phrase translated in the RSV as *umpire*. Unlike his friends, who advise a religious remedy, Job knows that self-medication is pointless (9:30). He needs someone who can lay his hands on both Job and God as a common friend, a negotiator (see Is 1:18)—not a judge who would decide his case. Strahan observes "that while Job is ostensibly pleading for justice, deep down he is seeking for reconciliation, and finds here an unconscious prophecy of incarnation and atonement" (Rowley, *The Book of Job,* p. 82).

In all of this there are two redeeming features to Job's spiritual quest. First, he views God as essentially unmanageable. Bildad can apply cause-effect logic to the science of knowing God (8:4-5); Job knows he must learn to live with mystery and will never know more than the "outer fringe of his works" (26:14). Job fears God (1:8). Second, while the friends watch and talk, Job explores God's ways.

Questions 9-10. In an important passage in his commentary, Francis Andersen notes:

> The gospel of Christ has not brought to any man a guarantee of less misery than Job's. It has brought rather the sharing of Christ's sufferings (Phil. 3:10), without which a person is but half a Christian. . . . And every distinguished forerunner of Christ in the Old Testament had to become 'a man of sorrows' (Is. 53:3)—Abraham, Jacob, Joseph, Moses, Ruth, Hannah, David, Hosea, Jeremiah—the list is long. Job is in this succession, and there is something he will find out about God as his Saviour which is much more than protection from harm or rescue from trouble. It is much more important for God to be with him in his trouble. This is what he is seeking in prayer. (*Job,* pp. 152-53)

Study 5. Job 13:1—14:17. The Faith That Rebels.
Purpose: To discover the place of godly rebellion in the life of faith.
Question 1. Derek Kidner notes that Job feels under attack from two quarters at once: from his God and his friends. Job is hurt that his friends concern themselves with what he has done (on the assumption that he is suffering as a

sinner) rather than what *God* has done. In response Job has reproached (6:26) and accused (13:4, 7-8) them. Eventually, he will mock them (21:3), hold them in contempt (21:34). But he does hold a pastoral concern for them, as evidenced in 13:7-11, a pastoral concern that finds its consummation, ironically, in his eventual prayer for their restoration to God (42:8-9). He proves to be their friend in the end in spite of their failure to be his. While Job is discovering the self-interest of his so-called friends, Job's friendship with God is being tested and proven to be remarkably free from self-interest (23:10).

Question 2. Undoubtedly the friends attack Job (11:6) because his pain threatens them (6:21; 18:3). They too could be similarly afflicted and need some rational basis of assuring themselves "that it couldn't happen to them." Mason says, "Job's comforters succeed only in twisting the knife in the wound and if you try to tell them that this is what they are doing to you, they will tactfully remind you that you are the one with the problem" (*Gospel According to Job*, p. 149). But there is further, deeper reason. Their theology does not explain how the Job they knew could suffer—unless he was a sinner in some way they had not known before.

They will be soon in the sad situation of feeling a secret pleasure when they discover that Job is worse than everyone thinks, and then they will bear the secret pain of discovering that their accusations of some hidden sin were entirely unfounded. Andersen notes that "Zophar falls into the common evangelistic error of applying the categories of guilt and pardon to every human problem" (*Job*, p. 158). Their rational, cause-effect theology may in the end be an intellectual idol, like the gods who have mouths but do not speak, feet but cannot walk (Ps 115:4-7). People who give their supreme loyalty to an inflexible, though manageable, theology will undoubtedly become inflexible. But those who worship the Lord, who "does whatever he pleases" (Job 23:13; Ps 115:3), will themselves be moveable and surprising people.

Question 3. What Job needs is not a theological treatise but flesh and blood friends with empathetic hearts. Indeed, sometimes the wisest thing to say is nothing (13:5)! Talking about God to a suffering person is in itself never enough. Better, as Job well knows, to talk to God.

Question 4. As the drama unfolds, Job is not reacting as Satan had assumed. He does not now say, "I have given up my belief in the goodness of God. I will stop worshiping God. I will curse God and die." Rather, he rebels against his friends' inadequate theology—a theology that nevertheless represents the best wisdom of the day. He rebels against any "explanation" that requires him to be untruthful about himself in order to be honest with God. He rebels against inventing sins to satisfy his confessors. He rebels against the idea that suffering is God's last word. He rebels against the notion that his righteousness—so deeply witnessed in his own heart, though he knows not why—is a creation of his own pride rather than a gift of God. He rebels against the silence of God, believing that God does speak, God will speak, and God will speak to him (14:15). While he once wanted to be left in peace, he will now fight his way through to a restored friendship with God.

The friends have a part to play, but not what they intended. Their judging spirits initially drive Job to break the downward spiral of despair (chapter 3) in his fascination with the idea of his own death. Further, their moralistic theology compels him to justify himself, not in the improper sense of establishing one's own righteousness apart from relationship to God on the basis of performance and religious activity, but rather in the biblical sense of the attributed, given righteousness of those who "fear God and shun evil" (1:8). This is also the New Testament sense, where those who have faith in the grace of Jesus Christ and his sufficient work on the cross (Gal 2:15-21) are justified even while being sinners.

Question 5. In so speaking Job reveals that his trust in God is unconditional, contrary to Satan's original taunt. Mason notes that there are probably only two other places in the Bible where such faith is expressed: Abraham's willingness to sacrifice his only son Isaac, and the willing death of the Son of God on the cross (*Gospel According to Job*, p. 154).

Question 6. It is not entirely clear what "two things" Job wants (13:20)! In the context Job is asking for several things: Job asks for the situation in which he can speak freely with God and bring his case forward. His intent is not merely "to argue his case" (13:3) in order to win his suit but, as the Hebrew word suggests, to reconcile the offended party by sorting out the misunderstanding. The word is used in this sense in Isaiah 1:18. As it is, Job feels intimidated and overpowered by his suffering and by God's awesome power. Job's God is so much bigger than the puny little god of Eliphaz, Bildad and Zophar, a god small enough to fit in the human brain. But Job also wants God to find something wrong with him—if he can! Most of all, he wants God to stop hiding from him and treating him as an enemy (13:24-28).

Question 7. As the passage in 14:1-6 indicates, Job thinks that one human life is too pitiful to be worth God's persistent *negative* attention. There seems to be more hope for a tree, which at least can be resuscitated into life. But whether there is any hope beyond the grave for a human being is indeed an issue (14:14) we will take up in the next question.

Question 8. Job is expressing the strongest confidence in both God's justice and his own innocence. Further, he is convinced that there is a hope worth considering beyond the grave. In spite of the attempts of some scholars to prove the opposite, the text suggests that Job is "playing" with the idea of life after death, first by considering the power of a tree to be rejuvenated (14:7-9)—unlike the dried lake that is never rejuvenated (14:11-12)—and second by his daring thought that after his service is rendered (presumably in the place of the dead) he will be renewed (14:14). Job considers that if God will long for his creature and will be sorry for killing Job, God will have to find some way of covering Job's sin (14:16-17).

The Old Testament hope of continuing personal existence after death was a distinctive feature of the faith of Israel. In continuity with the Old Testament Paul proclaims that the future of the Christian person is a "spiritual body" (1 Cor 15:44) like that of Jesus—a full human existence expressed bodily. This much we share with Job. But the Christian hope is invigorated by the fact that, with the coming of Jesus, the kingdom has *already* come, though not yet fully. So we taste the powers of the age to come. Even death has lost its sting. We do not have resurrection life fully now—contrary to what some Corinthians were saying—but we do not go down to the grave, as Job contemplated, uncertain about the other side or unable to live now in the light of that glorious future. Job lived with a hope that was essentially "not yet," but in Christ we live with the tension of "now" and "not yet."

Questions 9-10. Sometimes our attempt to defend God turns out to be a disservice to God, as Job points out in the case of his friends (13:7). He challenges them about showing God partially, covering up the enormity of what God has allowed or caused! Job's apologetic is crucial for our own (and others') journey of faith. Job proposes that in defending God we run the risk of deceit—covering up God's apparent injustices. In Job's refusal to defend God—a rebellion of sorts, but a rebellion in faith—Job offers by example the final apologetic for God—speaking with him oneself. "But I desire to speak to the Almighty and to argue my case with God" (13:3).

"Job is being tested. It is essential that he does not know why. He must ask why. He must test and reject all the answers attempted by men. In the end he will find satisfaction in what God himself tells him" (Andersen, *Job*, p. 125).

Study 6. Job 16:7—17:3; 19:23-27. Our Heavenly Guarantor.
Purpose: To learn about the grounds upon which a person can be confident that God is *for* them.

Question 1. The great moments of faith-discovery in this book, of which this chapter contains one, shine all the more brightly against the dark backdrop of

Job's suffering. Job piles image upon image of God's negative behavior toward him. He is a ferocious beast (16:9), a traitor (16:11), a wrestler (16:12), an archer (16:12-13), a swordsman (16:13-14) (Andersen, *Job,* p. 180).

Verse 10 is an obvious parallel to the suffering servant of Isaiah 50:6 and 53:3. It is God who turns Job over to evil men (his friends) for purposes unknown to the servant, but it is ultimately for God's glory and the accomplishment of God's purpose. Modern people might be more comfortable to say that "it happened" without direct reference to God's agency. That might make explanation easier, but it would lead to a reduced God and reduced faith. Andersen notes that the description of Job's suffering at the hand of God does not include any indication that Job fought back, admitted that his punishment was well-deserved or judged that God could be placated through a sacrifice (*Job,* p. 182). He sits in the dust in sackcloth but not because he is penitent. He is grieving, not repentant—not yet.

Question 2. In spite of his friends' accusations Job is convinced he comes to God with clean hands (11:13-15), partly because he has not cursed his companions.

Question 3. As with the Redeemer or Vindicator of 19:25, the identity of the "witness in heaven" (16:19) is somewhat uncertain. The difficulty is further complicated by the fact that the witness/intercessor pleads on behalf of God and Job at the same time. But as H. H. Rowley asserts, "It is to God that shed blood cries, and the psychological penetration of the struggle between two conceptions of God in Job's mind is greater than trust in a second heavenly figure" (*Book of Job,* p. 121). What is certain is that Job can find a defense in heaven. "With that unresolved tension between the God of his past experience, and the God of his present experience he appeals to God against himself, and proclaims his faith that the God he has known is still his Witness in heaven against the God who so torments him" (ibid., p. 116).

What Job cannot envision, and what constitutes the breathtaking message of the New Testament, is that God should provide within his own loving Trinity the means of reconciling his creature to himself, supplying in himself the intercession to himself which no human being is fit to offer, doing for his creature what only God can. The ultimate answer to the unresolved tension in Job's faith is the full trinitarian revelation of God in Jesus Christ through the Spirit. But even that must be held as mystery and not as a manageable doctrine about a God who can be fully defined in mental terms.

Question 5. Job's question is profound: Who else can put up security for our lives? If we cannot control our circumstances, the principalities and powers around us, or other human beings with similar powers as ourselves, it will take a heavenly guarantor to secure our future. Just as a more affluent, powerful person will pledge his superior assets on behalf of a weaker one, so Job dares to ask God to act as his guarantor. Already he has stumbled on a heavenly friend, intercessor and witness. But now he asks God to defend him against God! To give to God what God requires. Which is exactly what God in Christ did, the One in whom all the promises of God find their yes (2 Cor 1:20).

Question 6. The acknowledged climax of the whole book is the well-known affirmation "I know that my Redeemer lives" (19:25)—an assertion all the more audacious because it comes in the context of feeling betrayed by friends and devastated by God. Many scholars question this verse and the ones following. But, in spite of the textual difficulties, the main points are wonderfully clear: (1) Job is so certain of his innocence that he will commit to writing a record of his life. (2) He will see God (three times mentioned)—something more wonderful than hearing his voice. (3) He will see God in the flesh as a real human being. (4) His redeemer is God himself, thus resolving a notch farther the tension noted in the comments on question 5. (5) God the Redeemer will act on Job's behalf. There is enough here to warm the cockles of the heart and to evoke faith in the heart of the most beleaguered saint. What is not so certain is whether Job will see God after he has died (and has been resurrected) or before. Most probably it is the former, for reasons which Andersen outlines (*Job*, p. 194).

Question 7. The idea of a redeemer comes from the Hebrew understanding of the solidarity of the family. The redeemer or kinsman is a brother, father or cousin who is involved in everything one does, sharing guilt or avenging an enemy. Scriptural examples abound (Num 5:8; Deut 25:5; Ruth 3:9; 2 Sam 21). That God himself should become Job's nearest relative and vindicate him forever—on whichever side of the grave he might be—is surely the highest point of revelation in this book, and can be rightly called "The Gospel According to Job." It will take the New Testament to fully develop what that Redeemer must do—taking our place, suffering for us, defending our integrity and making us a son or daughter in God's family.

Question 8. Hope and faith belong together, as the frequent mention of "faith, hope and love" in the New Testament attests. Hope is not mere human wishing (as is suggested by our normal use of "hope" in sentences like "I hope to see you tomorrow"). Hope is based on the promises of God, on the character of God, on the record of God's deeds in history. But this hope that saves us is not hope based on what is seen (Rom 8:24), that is, based on verifiable evidence that is convincing without the exercise of faith. Therefore, Paul says we wait for it patiently—as Job did—experiencing the pleading of the Spirit's intercession in our hearts (Rom 8:26-27) and responding wholeheartedly to all that we know of God. In this way the basis of Job's and our hope is like the resurrection of Jesus, which was not a self-evident fact that convinced friend and enemy against their wills and without faith. Instead, as Jesus prophesied, the resurrection would only convince people who were already obeying the word they already had from God (Lk 16:31). Job is a case in point. He was ready to receive this hope because he was acting on what he already knew about God, especially his hunch that God wanted to be his friend.

Study 7. Job 20:1-19; 21:1-16. The Problem of Pain.
Purpose: To explore the potential and the limitations of a rational explanation for the problem of suffering.
Question 1. After reflecting on Job's retort, which Zophar considers to be an insult, Zophar elaborates on his view that the success of the wicked is both brief and self-destructive (v. 15). The death of the wicked will be swift (v. 8) and premature (v. 11). Zophar moves a little closer to Job's position, newly gained in the last study, that the final solution for the justice of God in the affairs of the world may not be found on this side of the grave. Zophar is discovering "that confidence in God's justice is not based on observation, but is a matter of trust and hope" (Andersen, *Job*, p. 196).
Question 3. Zophar still has no place in his theology for the suffering of the righteous and the innocent. Zophar and his friends operate on the assumption that sin produces suffering and that suffering proves sin.
Question 5. Job's speech in chapter 21 is the least prayerful (it is directed to the friends) and the most dialogical (it answers point by point the arguments of his friends, unlike his other speeches). For example, Eliphaz earlier stated that Job's tent would be safe if he were righteous (5:24); Job, now homeless, observes that the houses or tents of the wicked are secure (21:9). Bildad maintained that the wicked die childless (18:19); Job, having lost all his family, observes that the wicked have large, happy families (21:11). Zophar has just affirmed that the wicked die prematurely (20:11); Job, looking with both fear and fascination at his own imminent death, observes that the wicked live long and seem to get healthier as the years go by (21:7)! Some of the statements made by Job in this passage—obviously the opposite of what Job believes—are apparently quotations from his friends (v. 19). In the end (21:34) Job rejects their consolation as nonsense that, in face of reality, is blatantly false. The ultimate answer while not really an "answer" is found in God's speech in the whirlwind (Job 38—41). See the note on question 8.
Question 7. Known only to the reader is that the sufferings were brought on

at the instigation of Satan. This, however, does not explain Job's suffering. In fact Satan never appears again in the book and is never cited by Job, the friends or God as the source of human suffering. Further, and still unknown to Job, there are passages in the Bible that postpone resolving the questions about how God is managing the world until the end of history—and beyond. Job is not ready for a full eschatological (end-times) answer yet. But Job has made significant progress in his journey.

Job has stopped requiring everything to be worked out this side of the grave. He has a witness in heaven (16:19) and now believes he will see his Redeemer-Kinsman in a real human existence, though probably after he has died. He will sink again into despair, weary of his friends' pestering preaching and wondering about his own unrelieved suffering. But he now knows that the "answer" to the problem of pain is more than theological; it involves relationship with a caring God who, in the end, will not turn his back on him.

One of the answers Job will eventually test, initially raised by Eliphaz (5:17) but expounded later by the young man Elihu (36:10), is that suffering is a chastening of God for our moral and spiritual improvement. While this theme is suggested elsewhere in the Bible (Ps 94:12; Prov 3:11; Heb 12:5), it falls short of a full answer to Job's (or anyone else's) suffering and is not mentioned by God in the whirlwind speeches. Abraham's test (Gen 22), a case in point, is rightly considered a miniature book of Job (Andersen, *Job*, p. 125). Abraham's suffering was initiated by God but was neither a punishment for his sins nor a corrective measure for his improvement. Yet it was an experience that enlarged his faith in God and changed his life forever. In the same vein Andersen notes that the full biblical answer to the problem of pain is that God can and does actually transform evil into good "so that in retrospect (but only in retrospect!) it is seen to have actually been good, without diminishing in the least the awful actuality of the evil it was at the time" (ibid., p. 69). The final answer given in the Bible to the problem of pain is the cross of Jesus where God finally and completely transforms evil into good and personally, as a suffering God, bears the pain of his own creature redemptively.

Question 8. Speaking of Job's response to God's final "answer" to the problem of pain given in the whirlwind speech, Gustavo Gutiérrez says: "The truth [Job] has grasped and that has lifted him to the level of contemplation is that justice alone does not have the final say about how we are to speak of God. Only when we have come to realize that God's love is freely bestowed do we enter fully and definitely into the presence of the God of faith" (*On Job*, p. 87).

Zophar wants a theology that makes the sun shine only on the righteous. Job sees the wicked receiving God's blessing and the righteous receiving pain. He is not convinced that Zophar's mechanical cause-effect theology is right, and he is exploring through prayer an alternative. Eventually, he will be ready to declare that God gives generously without respect to the worthiness of the recipient. The drama started with Satan's question "Does Job fear God for nothing?" Now the drama is moving to a deeper, though related, question: "Does God give his love and blessing for nothing?" Put in other words, the fundamental question of the book may be framed, "Is God so good that he can be loved simply for himself and not for his gifts?" That question can be explored in the context of the question "Are human beings so loved by God that God will care for them regardless of their behavior and worthiness?"

Question 9. This final question is probed helpfully in *Search the Scriptures*: "In this second cycle Job's friends, gaining no victory, utter threats. Is defeated conservatism bound to take refuge in acid predictions of gloom? Had Job something to teach them if only they were willing to listen?" (Alan M. Stibbs, ed., rev. ed. [London: Inter-Varsity Press, 1969], p. 227).

Study 8. Job 23. The Silence of God.
Purpose: To explore the silence of God as a loving invitation to honest prayer and communion.

Questions 1-2. Job's friends want Job to repent of his sins. Job's problem is this: he admits he is a sinner (19:4), but he cannot account for his suffering by errors on his part.

Job wants to present his case personally to God. Given the opportunity, he believes he could convince God that he is truly righteous (v. 4)—the very thing God already knows, though this fact is unknown to Job (1:8)! Earlier he cringed at the thought of a face-to-face confrontation. Now he desires such a meeting, not only because his pilgrimage has led him to the conviction that he has a friend and relative in heaven, but also because he now wants God even more than he wants answers to his questions. On the one hand this seems to be the height of self-righteousness, especially when one realizes that the acceptance he seeks is not the pardon of a guilty man by grace but the acquittal of a righteous man by law (Andersen, *Job*, p. 209). On the other hand this hunger for justification seems entirely in the mainstream of true biblical spirituality.

Job feared God and shunned evil even by the Lord's own assessment (1:8). Job could point positively, as he later does, to his stunning record in chapter 29 (rejoicing in the light of God's presence and loving the poor and powerless) and negatively in chapter 31 (shunning the full catalog of sins of spirit, mind and body). This is no mere salvation by works but is entirely in line with the Pauline doctrine of justification by faith, a principle to which both the law and prophets point (Rom 3:21). The fear of God, as the wisdom poem (Job 28:1-28) indicates, is a holy marriage of reverence for God and morality in life (28:28). In New Testament terms it is faith active in love.

Questions 3-4. Verses 8 and 9 tell us that Job does not know where to go to find God. But there is a deeper reason for God's apparent unavailability. Just as Jesus delayed going to Bethany when he heard of Lazarus's illness (Jn 11:5-6) because of his love for him, so God withholds the full experience of his presence for reasons only partly known to us. John White notes that "we confuse intimacy with its counterfeit, familiarity. Intimacy is what we want but familiarity is all we achieve. Intimacy is dangerous, a knowing and a being known deeply and profoundly" (*Daring to Draw Near* [Downers Grove, Ill.: InterVarsity Press, 1977], p. 100).

Question 5. Blaise Pascal said that to search for God is to know that you have already been found by him! So the true pilgrim speaks more of being known by God (Ps 139:1; Gal 4:9) than of knowing God. That indeed is Job's hope: God knows him better than his friends do!

Questions 6-7. Andersen notes that Job holds together two opposites: the consciousness of an intimate personal relationship with God by walking in God's ways (lining his life up with God's commands and wisdom, v. 11) and a vivid awareness that he is currently being denied fellowship with God (*Job*, p. 209). So Job has lived by fearing God and shunning evil (the Old Testament equivalent of living by Spirit and Word) even without the attending confirmation of the nearness of God. But that obedience is itself a prayer, a prayer that will eventually be answered in a way chosen by God. Simone Weil spoke to this: "For us, this obedience in relation to God is what the transparency of a window pane is in relation to light. As soon as we feel this obedience with our whole being, we see God" (*Waiting on God* [London: Collins, 1950], p. 89). In other words God is not entirely silent since he has given us wisdom and Scripture. His seeming silence and our waiting are the fertile ground for faith. When and if God so chooses, faith will become sight, if not on this side of the grave, at least on the other.

Question 8. The Hebrew text here has been variously interpreted, but it seems best to understand *way* in verse 10 not as Job's way but as God's way taken by Job (Andersen, *Job*, p. 210): "God knows his way with me."

Job is coming to the place where he could live without an answer for his suffering because he is convinced that God knows that he is walking in the steps of the Lord (v. 11). Therefore the test he is undergoing is not the purification process of removing the dross but the testing to prove that Job himself is pure gold in God's sight—the very thing Job has maintained from the start! This is not self-righteousness but the boldness of true faith. Job is an Old Testament prototype of the true gospel believer who dares to come to God just as he is because—as we learn in the New Testament—of an imputed, given righteousness through faith in God's Son and our Messiah, Jesus.

Questions 9-10. Compared with the puny God of Job's friends, Job's God is completely unmanageable: "He does whatever he pleases." Job's God cannot be tamed (see 12:13-25), and therefore cannot be manipulated into giving justice. That is both Job's problem and his hope. As we will soon see when God reveals himself to Job in the whirlwind (chapters 38—41), Job's final "answer" is found in the revelation of a God so great that the only appropriate response is worship. John White says, "The problem of suffering remains incompletely solved in the book, but for Job it no longer existed. It is not just that his fortunes were restored again. A greater richness had come into his life, the richness a man knows when he treasures the majesty and glory of God" (*Daring to Draw Near,* p. 109).

Study 9. Job 35; 36:13-16. Songs in the Night.

Purpose: To show the futility of trying to explain specific situations in people's lives by appealing to general theological principles.

General note. The four speeches of Elihu (32:1—37:24) are sometimes thought to add nothing to the discussion. Job does not even respond to Elihu. God doesn't mention Elihu when he comments negatively on the ministry of the friends (42:7). But Elihu does add something to the discussion, and his speeches form an important transition from the defiant Job to the God who speaks in the storm. Elihu's vision of the awesomeness of God in nature (36:27—37:24) makes him one who "prepares the way of the Lord" who speaks in chapters 38—41 in terms of his exquisite joy in creation.

Question 1. Elihu's God is distant and impartial—not affected by human action, whether good or evil. The result of such a view is human indifference. Rational answers to the problem of pain will always leave the heart cold. That Elihu's theology is an expression of his own cold heart is indicated by the curse he calls down on Job: "Oh, that Job might be tested to the utmost for answering like a wicked man!" (34:36).

Question 2. It is the wicked, Job says, who ask, "What would we gain by praying to him?" (21:15). Unknown to both Job and Elihu, Satan asked this question as well (1:9-10). So Elihu infers that this is what is bothering Job, while all along Job's deepest concern is not with what he gets out of being righteous but what has happened to his relationship with God. Elihu misses this because he is determined to uphold the honor and justice of God. Elihu believes that human righteousness does not affect God at all (v. 7). God, in this man's view, is neither delighted with a good man nor grieved with an evil man, since God is an impartial administrator (34:19). In so speaking of God he believes he is defending God's honor, but in fact he is defending his own theology.

Question 5. This question *was* asked by Job, over and again. It was Job's obsession. More than anything—even any *thing*—Job wanted God, God's fellowship, God's Word, God's approval, God's presence.

The range of answers supplied by the friends are similar to those heard today: "not enough faith," "unconfessed sin" (v. 12), "you are not praying right" (v. 16). Elihu, and his modern counterparts, can deal with unanswered prayer with a handy formula: God answers those who pray correctly. How could God answer Job's prayers that are so ignorant (v. 16)? For Elihu there is no mystery to God's work. Like the three other friends, he has God well managed. But he is unable to "manage" Job's predicament any better than his older friends. Job, in contrast, "lives in the suspense of faith, praying without guarantees" (Andersen, *Job*, p. 258).

Question 6. Elihu does bring an important emphasis—he talks about what we can learn from suffering. It is not entirely absent from the previous speeches but now is drawn out more explicitly. If, as C. S. Lewis once observed, God whispers to us in our pleasures, he shouts at us in our pain. Elihu says something similar in the passage next to be studied: "he speaks to them in their affliction" (36:15). This may relate to Elihu's most beautiful contribution to the discussion, his reference to God giving us "songs in the night" (35:10)—surely a hint of God's graciousness in an otherwise cheerless lecture.

Question 7. Nowhere does the Bible actually speak of "the patience of Job." The New Testament refers to Job's *perseverance*, not his patience: "You have heard of Job's perseverance and have seen what the Lord finally brought about" (Jas 5:11). Certainly if patience means lying down, biting the tongue and keeping a stiff upper lip when things go wrong, Job was anything but patient. He held out passionately with stubborn persistence to gain consolation from God. The essence of his faith was insistence on a personal encounter with God. Mike Mason says, "Many Christians are so preoccupied with trying to be patient that the more rugged, energetic, visionary side of patience—what the Bible calls perseverance—has been leeched out of their character" (*Gospel According to Job*, p. 364).

Question 9. The search for an answer to Job's suffering by finding a sufficient cause has failed. Elihu's fourth speech (36:1—37:24) makes an important transition from cause-effect theology to mystery. Elihu now moves in the direction God will take up—so much more redemptively—when God finally speaks: the direction of the gratuitiveness of God. God does not despise people (36:5-12). Indeed he uses trouble to train people in righteousness—a use that makes even adversity somewhat sweet (v. 15), so sweet that they can hear or sing songs in the night (a metaphor of God's comfort in the most cheerless time). While it is true that the person who refuses to pray when in trouble comes to a shameful and untimely end (36:13-14), God is actually wooing people in affliction to himself. Elihu uses the Hebrew expression that would be used by a young man pleading for the heart of his beloved (35:16). Though Elihu makes a positive contribution to the discussion, it pales before the direct revelation of God to Job that will follow.

Study 10. Job 38:1-11, 31-41; 40:1-5. God in the Storm.
Purpose: To understand God's response to Job—knowing God is more important than getting answers to our moral dilemmas.
Questions 1-2. The range of creatures noted by God in chapters 38 and 39 is a significant sample. God's deluge of questions relating to these creatures does not seem to have anything to do with why Job has suffered so severely. But to begin with, the use of questions by God is significant. They are, as Andersen notes, not a way of making a pronouncement but are "invitations, suggestions about discoveries he will make as he tries to find his own answers" (*Job*, p. 269). They are educative in the true sense—not meant to humiliate Job but to call him to learn in God's schoolroom, the world. The world, Job will be led to see, is not, as moderns so proudly assume, created for humankind, for our pleasure and exploitation. Just the reverse: we were made *for* the world—to take care of it (Gen 2:5, 15). But even more surprising, the world was, we now realize, made for God's glory and pleasure, as witnessed by God's reminder that God makes grass and flowers to grow and flourish on the distant moors "where no man lives" (38:26). By a barrage of carefully crafted questions God brings Job to the place of knowing that he is not the creator of the world. He wasn't even around at the time!
Question 4. God emphasizes what Job cannot do, rather than what he can do as an awesome God-imaging creature. In another section of the poem, God reminds Job that God makes rain fall and grass grow in places where no human will ever tread. We might have appreciated hearing how humankind can tame certain animals. God wants us to know that only God can make a wild donkey (39:5-8).

God's obvious enjoyment of his own creation is one of the subtle messages of the book. Not so subtle is the fact that Job will get along with himself better if he is rightly related *both* to the Creator and the creation, a principle largely lost in modern life, which encourages relationship either exclusively to the creation (parts of the environmental movement) or to the Creator (the spirituality movement). These beautiful poems about goats and ostriches, constellations and sea monsters (probably the crocodile) are right on target: it is as a person in the world among other creatures that Job will find answers to his questions, and if not, the capacity to live with joy when his questions remain unanswered.

Question 5. The passage begins with a misunderstood phrase: "Who is this that darkens my counsel?" (v. 2). *Counsel* usually refers to the plan and providence of God, something which God will declare Job spoke well about (42:8). The meaning is apparently that Job is in the dark, having received the advice ("knowledge") dispensed by the wise men around him (his friends). Now God will bring his own light to Job's problem (Andersen, *Job,* pp. 273-74). Presumably Job will draw some conclusions about his creatureliness: he did not exist from the beginning of time; he cannot be everywhere at once; he cannot endow the heart with wisdom (v. 36) or discharge lightning bolts; he has not yet been through the death experience (v. 17). All of this is designed to help Job put his problems into perspective. He is, after all, a creature, not God. In spite of God's progressive whittling of Job down to size, there is no suggestion that God despises Job. Just the reverse. God invites Job to stand up like a man (38:3) and enter into dialogue with God. Francis Andersen notes:

> There is a kindly playfulness in the Lord's speeches which is quite relaxing. Their aim is not to crush Job with an awareness of his minuteness contrasted with the limitless power of God, not to mock him when he puts his tiny mind beside God's vast intellect. On the contrary, the mere fact that God converses with him gives him a dignity above all the birds and beasts, assuring him that it is a splendid thing to be a man. (*Job,* p. 271)

Question 7. It is important to catch the tone of the Lord's point. He is not trying to force Job to capitulate to God's superior wisdom. "Answer" does not imply "answering back" but something more friendly, indeed something ironical. If Job understands any of the matters above better than God himself, then God would be willing to learn from Job (Andersen, *Job,* p. 285)!

Question 8. In 21:5, responding to the friends' tirade, Job asked his friends to look on him with astonishment and clap their hands over their mouths to stem the tide of their inappropriate speech. Job recalls that before he was devastated by God, the chief men in the village would show their respect for Job by refraining from speaking—all the more unusual coming from the nobles (29:9). Now it is Job's turn. Job has no answer to God's questions. Mike Mason comments, "One can fall on one's face and yet continue to blubber and babble. But to yield the tongue is to yield everything [James 3:2]" (*Gospel*, p. 411).

Questions 9-10. Job has not necessarily submitted and repented (contrary to what some commentators suggest). He is respectfully silent, but the matter is not over. Apparently, the Lord sees it this way because he takes up his speech a second time. Not every complaint is a revolt. And blind, unthinking submission is not the hallmark of faith. But in every complaint there will be elements of nonfaith which, in the context of God's loving ministry, can be brought into harmony with his glory and purpose.

Jean-Pierre De Caussaude proposes: "To find contentment in the present moment is to relish and adore the divine will in the succession of all the things to be done and suffered which make up the duty to the present moment" (*The Sacrament of the Present Moment*, trans. Kitty Muggeridge [Glasgow: Collins, 1981], p. 84). Job is not there yet—and should not be rushed into a compliant grudging submission as an alternative to loving faith. Job wanted an audience to demonstrate in what an exemplary way he has run his life. What he got was a lecture on how well God runs the world. Job wanted deliverance from his judge (23:7). God speaks about how much he enjoys being judge. Job wanted God to look favorably on him—one special creature from the land of Uz. What Job got was an invitation to appreciate two of God's most splendid and uncontrollable creatures: the hippopotamus (40:15-24) and the crocodile (41:1-34). Job wanted to prove his innocence. God proved Job's littleness. Job wanted an intimate conversation with his friend in heaven (29:4). God gave him poetry and some hymns of praise.

Study 11. Job 40:6-14; 42:1-6. The Joy of Repentance.
Purpose: To deepen our understanding and experience of repentance as a positive and life-giving posture.

Question 1. In 40:4-5 Job has nothing to say (the hand clapped over the mouth), but he has not yet admitted his sin. And God's resumption into a second speech is a further loving ministry to bring Job to peace with God, himself and the entire created order. Job is not defiant but still has not gotten the point, a point that God probes both by direct questioning (vv. 6-14) and indirect analogies (40:7—41:34). Were Job already repentant and submissive God could get on with others matters. Martin Buber said that real self-knowledge

Leader's Notes _____ 91

leads a person either to self-destruction or to rebirth (as quoted in Raines, *Creative Brooding*, p. 14). It is a perilous moment.

Question 2. Without intending so, Job has been discrediting and condemning God by insisting that his own view of the moral structure of the world is the right one. By Job's view God is not living up to his own highest morality: he lets the wicked get off scot-free and allows the righteous (like himself) to go through hell on earth. Without saying so, he implies that if God is God, he is not good. If he were good he would approve of Job's righteousness against the condemning sneer of his friends. So Job refuses to repent of sins—the sins dreamed up by his friends to "justify" his obvious experience of God's punishments ("I will maintain my righteousness and never let go of it" [27:6]). *And in this Job was right!* Indeed he never is required by God to repent of the friends' "list." But while he need not repent of sins, he must get a deeper grasp of sin—the root problem. To do this God must expand his horizons so he can repent willingly and gladly rather than reluctantly and dismally.

Question 4. The theme of Job's integrity (righteousness) runs through the entire book. It is that amazing sense of standing before God without shame and enjoying God's approval even though, as Job knew all too well, we are still sinners (7:20). Job was a gospel-believer before the time of Christ, anticipating the righteousness that comes through faith rather than performance. Grasping this—and being grasped by it—is the heart of conversion to Christ. Martin Luther, wrestling with how a just God could accept sinners, suddenly discovered in his study of Romans that the justice of God is that act of God on the cross of Christ by which he *justifies* the ungodly. And to him, as for us, the gates of heaven opened and he felt as one born again.

Question 5. Verses 7-14 are the heart of the Lord's reply to Job and are significantly placed between the two nature speeches. The problem of putting God in the wrong in order to prove Job in the right is placed in a much larger moral context. In these verses Job is reminded that only if Job had the right of humbling the proud and crushing the evil—the right to exercise God's judgment—could God allow Job to vindicate himself (vv. 11-14). Some help in understanding this is given by knowing how justice worked in Hebrew society. The judge gave the verdict, passed sentence and secured the right of the injured party. "It was only indirectly, in connection with restoring things to rights, that wrongdoers were punished" (Andersen, *Job*, p. 286).

What God wants Job to admit is this: as a creature he does not have the ability to administer his own justice or to vindicate himself. God's references to his own power in creation are fundamental to this. The two nature poems in 40:15—41:34 (the behemoth is possibly the hippopotamus and the leviathan is possibly the crocodile) indicate two creatures that a human being would find impossible to tame, a fact significant to Job's underlying problem. Verse 9 says, "Do you have an arm like God's?" To take over the moral administration of the universe Job would have to be as powerful as God. Job knows this, but he has not been able, thus far, to accept the Lord's administration of the world without fretting, without complaining, without reservation. He is struggling to let God be God, and this brings us to the heart of his repentance.

Question 7. With considerable depth Francis Andersen comments on the theology of the book at this point.

> There is a rebuke in [this book] for any person who, by complaining about particular events in his life, he could propose to God better ways of running the universe than those God currently uses. Men are eager to use force to combat evil and in their impatience they wish God would do the same more often. But by such destructive acts men do and become evil. To behave as God suggests in 40:8-14, Job would not only usurp the role of God, he would become another Satan. Only God can destroy creatively. Only God can transmute evil into good. As Creator, responsible for all that happens in His world, He is able to make everything (good and bad) work together into good. The debate has been elevated to a different level. The reality of God's goodness lies beyond justice. That is why the categories of guilt and punishment, true and terrible though they are can only view human suffering as a consequence of sin, not as an occasion of grace. (*Job,* pp. 287-88)

Job has an expanded view of the world, seeing himself as a creature simultaneously relating to the Creator and other creatures. God's power and glory throb through it all. He cannot control God, not even in his theology. Job now has moved from "hearsay" evidence for God to firsthand encounter—"seeing" God (42:5) as few other saints have. He knows his Redeemer lives (19:25). He has unrestrained admiration for God (42:2). What he confesses at this point is not his list of sins but the greatness of God.

Question 8. Getting to the heart of Job's repentance is crucial, not only for a clear understanding of how the story really ends but for our own relationship with God. It is quite apparent that Job never capitulates to his friends' spiritual direction to repent of his sins. It would be dishonest to do so, and God does not require it.

What happens in Job's heart is more fundamental. Just as the "sins" of Romans 1:22-32 are mere symptoms (expressed in different ways in different people) of the root sin of irreverence and ingratitude (Rom 1:21), so the root of Job's problem is found in his impoverished worship of God. He needs to repent *to* reverence and gratitude. Job cannot make himself grovel by mere introspection or by succumbing to the judgment of other creatures. Such groveling can turn out merely to be another form of self-help "works" with no faith in it. It might even be the cloak of pride turned inside out. Instead of being repentance it might be remorse, shame or even false guilt. True repentance is not worked up from below but inspired from above. And Job cannot repent until he meets God. When he does meet God he *wants* to repent, not of some puny list of things done that should not have been done, or things not done that should have been (he argues just the reverse in chapters 29—31). He repents of something more fundamental: of trying to be God, of pretending that he can think like God, of playing God.

Question 10. The translation "despise myself" is possibly inaccurate. *Myself* does not appear in the original Hebrew. Unquestionably Job is now a humble suppliant like Abraham (Gen 18:27), but he is not groveling in the sudden realization that his sins are almost innumerable and punishment will soon engulf him. His repentance involved self-depreciation in the deepest and healthiest sense of relinquishing a godlike presumption. His repentance involved welcoming his status as a creature, though never as a *mere* creature. Speaking to the distinction between healthy repentance and unhealthy self-disgust, John White says, "He is at peace who has seen himself appropriately placed in the total scheme of things" (*Daring to Draw Near,* p. 106).

Study 12. Job 42:7-17. Is Faith Always Worthwhile?
Purpose: To explore the message of Job as it relates to disinterested faith—faith *for* the love of God.

Questions 1-2. One of the strangest reversals of the book is God's assessment of the situation. The friends delivered conservative orthodox theology to the rebellious Job—and were judged for not speaking correctly about God. Job storms heaven with his prayers—vacillating between wanting an audience with God to prove his innocence and fearing that if he ever got such an audience he would be tongue-tied in terror—and God says Job spoke correctly!

Earlier we noted that while the friends spoke *about* God, Job spoke *to* God (in prayer). This is a crucial point. Job's "full encounter with his God came by way of complaint, bewilderment, and confrontation" (Gutiérrez, *On Job,* p. 55), but he got to God in the end because he prayed. In his prayer and desire to be with God, Job revealed his right belief in God. His friends had God theologically managed, but their God was a distant god of sterile rationalism. They represented the religious wisdom of Job's day.

Question 5. The book is full of ironies, some of which have already been discovered. Here is another: The friends who came to "comfort" Job in his misery (but failed to do so) are now in need of Job's patronage. It is surely one more indication of Job's "disinterested" faith, now deepened by his discovery of the free love of God given to good and evil, that he prays for his former accusers. "My servant Job will pray for you, and I will accept his prayer" (42:8).

Questions 7-8. Significantly, the restoration of his fortunes is not timed with his repentance but with his intercession for his friends. There is not a shred of evidence that the author of Job has slipped back, as some allege, into a crude theology of rewards and punishments—the very thing this book transcends in its central message. Early in the book, when Job first experienced excruciating loss, he blessed God (1:21) instead of cursing him, thus proving Satan wrong at least in the first test. Job did not need material prosperity to sustain his trust in God. After each trial, Job persists in his integrity. His faith is not inspired by the hope of material reward. As Gutiérrez notes, "It is thus made clear from the outset that gratuitiveness is a main characteristic of authentic faith in God" (*On Job*, p. 54). The gifts of God at the end—cattle, sons and daughters—were "gestures of grace, not rewards for virtue" (Andersen, *Job*, p. 294).

Question 10. Rational answers to the problem of pain have little place in the ministry to a suffering person asking, Why? What people need are friends, and listening friends at that! The ultimate question is not Why? but Who? The reason some people come to faith in God, or remain so, seems to have little to do with life, or their experience of life. Some who go through hard times—with no explanation—believe all the more; others become bitter. The difference has something to do with prayer and the God to whom they believe they are praying. Job is bitter against life but not bitter against God. He attributes all his suffering to God (even though the book does not) and yet he still cries out to God and wants God. Does Job fear God for his own salvation or justification? No, he does not think he is justified by God even though he feels that he is innocent, certainly innocent of all that his friends accuse him of. Mature faith in God is not *for* anything, not even for salvation, certainly not for earthly benefits. It is for God.

Question 11. In the last study we saw that Job had to repent of attempting to understand everything. "The truth that he has grasped and that has lifted him to the level of contemplation is that justice alone does not have the final say about how we are to speak of God. Only when we have come to realize that God's love is freely bestowed do we enter fully and definitively into the presence of the God of faith" (Gutiérrez, *On Job*, p. 87). Job must live with mystery.

So, in the end, Job loves God not for the reward but because God is God. This is all the more remarkable since this ancient saint apparently did not have the benefit of the covenant community of Israel, the memories of God's mighty acts in history and the revelation of God's purpose in the prophets. His whole experience contradicted the principle of loving God for his own sake. So it might truly be said, "Next to Jesus, Job must be the greatest *believer* in the whole Bible" (Andersen, *Job,* p. 271).

R. Paul Stevens *teaches at Regent College in Vancouver, British Columbia. He is also the author of the LifeBuilder Bible Studies* 1 Corinthians *(coauthored with Dan Williams),* 2 Corinthians, Revelation *and* End Times.